CONFEDERATE GENERALS

GENERALS

of

NORTH CAROLINA

CONFEDERATE GENERALS

GENERALS
_of_
NORTH CAROLINA

TAR HEELS IN COMMAND

JOE A. MOBLEY

Charleston · London

THE
History
PRESS

Published by The History Press
Charleston, SC 29403
www.historypress.net

All images courtesy of the North Carolina State Archives.

First published 2011

Manufactured in the United States

ISBN 978.1.60949.048.5

Mobley, Joe A.
Confederate generals of North Carolina : Tar Heels in command / Joe A. Mobley.
p. cm.
Includes bibliographical references.
ISBN 978-1-60949-048-5
1. Generals--Confederate States of America--Biography. 2. Generals--North Carolina-
-Biography. 3. Confederate States of America. Army--Officers--Biography. 4. North
Carolina--History--Civil War, 1861-1865--Biography. 5. United States--History--Civil War,
1861-1865--Biography. 6. United States--History--Civil War, 1861-1865--Campaigns.
7. North Carolina--Biography. I. Title.
E467.M69 2011
355.0092'2--dc23
[B]
2011029178

For Kay

Contents

Contents

Acknowledgements

I wish to express my appreciation to several individuals for their assistance in the completion of this volume. I am grateful to Elizabeth Crowder, who searched for images of North Carolina's Confederate generals, and to Kim Cumber and Andrea Gabriel of the North Carolina State Archives, Office of Archives and History, for the photographs from that institution that illustrate the book. I also thank David L.S. Brook, director of Historical Research at the Office of Archives and History, for pointing out the North Carolinians who served as generals in the Union army. I owe a note of thanks to my mentor and friend William C. Harris for his interest and advice, as well as to Jackson Marshall, an associate director at the North Carolina Museum of History, for reading a portion of the manuscript for accuracy. My greatest debt is to my wife, Kathleen B. (Kay) Wyche, who proofread and corrected the draft. As always, her patience, encouragement, advice, and editorial skill were indispensable.

Joe A. Mobley

Introduction

This book briefly recounts the careers of forty-six men who served as Confederate generals during the Civil War. All had ties to North Carolina. They were either born in the state or, if natives of other states, directly commanded North Carolina troops. Louis Addison Armistead is remembered in histories of the war for leading Virginia troops and for his dramatic death at Gettysburg. But he was born in the North Carolina town of New Bern, spent the first year of his life there, and had strong family attachments to the state. Therefore, he is included. Some generals, such as Alfred Iverson and William Henry Chase Whiting, were natives of other states but led North Carolina soldiers in battle. They also are presented here.

Among the forty-six generals, there were thirty-one brigadier generals, twelve major generals, two lieutenant generals, and one full general. Customarily, a brigadier general commanded a brigade. A major general led a division. A lieutenant general commanded a corps. A full general led an army.

A regiment usually consisted of ten companies. A similar unit having fewer than ten companies was commonly known as a battalion. A brigade was composed of four regiments, and at least two brigades made up a division. A corps was formed by two or more divisions, and an army comprised corps. The Confederate States Army had several component armies and departments—for example, the Army of Northern Virginia, the Army of Tennessee, and the Department of the Trans-Mississippi.

The method by which North Carolina regiments were organized and designated for Confederate service causes some confusion. A state law of May 8, 1861 (before North Carolina seceded from the Union), authorized the formation of ten regiments of North Carolina State Troops. General

James Green Martin became the state adjutant general for those troops. Simultaneously, under existing law, regiments of North Carolina Volunteers were formed. General John Franklin Hoke became state adjutant general for the Volunteers. In the summer, Hoke's position was abolished, and Martin became adjutant general for both the State Troops and the Volunteers.

Martin found himself saddled with a system whereby both organizations used the same numbers to designate their regiments. There were ten regiments of State Troops, named the First through the Tenth. And there were fourteen regiments of North Carolina Volunteers, called the First through the Fourteenth. Thus there were, for example, a First Regiment North Carolina State Troops and a First Regiment North Carolina Volunteers. That situation created confusion for both state and Confederate authorities. As a result, they decided that the State Troops regiments would retain their numbering of one through ten and that the Volunteers regiments would be renumbered, beginning with eleven. Thus the Volunteers would be designated the Eleventh through the Twenty-fourth Regiments North Carolina Troops, and all future North Carolina regiments, beginning with the Twenty-fifth, would be known as North Carolina Troops. To add further confusion, however, some of the state's cavalry and artillery regiments were also numbered as part of their branch of service. For example, the Ninth Regiment North Carolina State Troops was also known as the First Regiment North Carolina Cavalry.

Two native North Carolinians who held general rank temporarily are not described in this book because their service was brief and only tangential to the Tar Heel State. They did not receive commissions in the Confederate army but rather from the states of Georgia and Tennessee. John Lewis Sneed was born in Raleigh in 1820 but moved to Tennessee. During the war, he held for a short time the rank of brigadier in command of a camp for volunteers. Then the governor of Tennessee appointed him to oversee settlements between the Confederacy and the Tennessee provisional army. William Phillips was born in Asheville in 1824 but soon moved to Georgia. That state's governor appointed him a brigadier to command a training camp for volunteers. In August 1861, he resigned that position to become colonel of "Phillips's Legion." However, ill health forced him to resign and return to civilian life and to a short stint as a major in the Georgia Militia.

Over time, several North Carolinians have mistakenly been given the title of "General," presumably for Confederate service. Colonel William James Hoke, a Lincolnton merchant, has sometimes been confused with his brother, General John Franklin Hoke. Colonel Duncan Kirkland McRae—a lawyer, legislator, diplomat, and wartime foreign supply agent, as well as a regimental commander—has been mistaken occasionally for a general. Colonel George Washington Rains has been confused on occasion with his brother, General Gabriel James Rains. "General" Julian Shakespeare Carr, a wealthy North Carolina tobacco industrialist, saw a short period of service as a private in a North Carolina company. His honorary title appeared after the war, when he became commander of the United Confederate Veterans in the state. North Carolina legislator and congressman Alfred Dockery had the nickname "General," but there is no evidence that he ever undertook any military service. *The War of the Rebellion: A Compilation of the Official Records of the Union and Confederate Armies* briefly notes that "General Mann" promised to call out his Militia brigade in 1862. Possibly that was William E. Mann, a sheriff and publisher in Elizabeth City. Walter Clark's *Histories of the Several Regiments and Battalions from North Carolina in the Great War, 1861–'65* refers to Jesse R. Stubbs, a Martin County lawyer, legislator, and railroad president, as "General." But no record so far has been found to suggest that either Mann or Stubbs held such a commission during the war.

Although not technically members of the Confederate States Army, generals in the North Carolina Militia and Home Guard—appointed by the state—nevertheless served the Confederate cause and are included in this volume. North Carolina commissioned David Clark a brigadier general to command Militia in the northeastern part of the state and awarded the same rank to Collett Leventhorpe and John Wesley McElroy to command units of the Home Guard. Four North Carolinians—Daniel Gould Fowle, Richard Caswell Gatlin, John Franklin Hoke, and James Green Martin—served as state adjutants general, responsible for local defense and for organizing and supplying North Carolina troops for the war. To hold that office, they received commissions as generals of Militia from the state. Subsequently, Gatlin and Martin were also commissioned brigadier generals in the Confederate army.

Militia troops, organized into local companies, remained in the state for local defense, to help enroll conscripts (draftees), and to hunt Confederate deserters. But the militiamen themselves were subject to conscription (the draft) into regular regiments; only the officers were exempt. Therefore, in July 1863, the state dissolved the Militia and established the Guard for Home Defense. The former Militia officers then became officers in the new organization. The Home Guard, as it was known, took on the responsibilities that had formerly been those of the Militia. It included men between the ages of eighteen and fifty who were already exempt from Confederate service. It was organized into a battalion in each county, although four counties had only four companies each. Several regiments were formed in large counties. Some adjacent counties joined together to organize a regiment. Ultimately, there were nine regiments of the Home Guard. Some of its units drilled regularly and responded quickly to orders of deployment, and others did not drill and were called up only to defend their counties. The Home Guard's ranks were depleted, though, when its members were enrolled in Confederate service toward the end of the war. Also, the Confederate Congress in February 1864 authorized battalions and regiments of Reserves. The Senior Reserves consisted of men between forty-five and fifty years of age. The Junior Reserves were composed of boys seventeen years old.

Four North Carolinians served as generals in the Union army. Born in Raleigh, future U.S. president Andrew Johnson (1808–1875) received a Federal army commission as general when he became President Abraham Lincoln's military governor of Tennessee. Solomon Meredith (1810–1875) was born in Guilford County and migrated to Indiana at age nine. In that state, before the war, he served in the legislature and as a U.S. marshal. As a Union brigadier, he commanded the famed Iron Brigade in 1862–63. He received a brevet to major general in August 1865, the same month he was mustered out of the army. He accepted an appointment as government surveyor in Montana before retiring to his farm in Indiana. A native of Richmond County, Joseph Roswell Hawley (1826–1905) left the state at age eleven and settled in Connecticut. Before the war, he became a lawyer, a newspaper editor, a Free-Soiler, and an organizer of the Republican Party in that state. As a brigadier during the conflict, he commanded troops in New York to keep order in the elections of November 1864. He was brevetted major general in 1865 and was deployed at Wilmington, North Carolina, in the final weeks of the war. Afterward, he served in the U.S. House and Senate as a Republican. John Gibbon (1827–1896) was born in Philadelphia but moved to Charlotte, North Carolina, at an early age and grew up there. A graduate of the U.S. Military Academy at West Point, he commanded the famed Iron Brigade before Meredith assumed leadership. Gibbon subsequently rose to division and corps commander and was one of the Federal army commissioners receiving General Robert E. Lee's surrender at Appomattox Court House in April 1865. After the war, he gained the permanent rank of brigadier general and campaigned against Indians in the West.

Of North Carolina's forty-six Confederate generals, ten were killed or died of wounds in the war. Twenty-one were wounded but survived the conflict.

Six became prisoners of war. Without extensive medical records, it is difficult to judge the overall health of the generals. Some, such as Robert Ransom Jr., suffered from chronic health problems throughout their lives. But if they survived the war, most enjoyed a relatively long lifespan, considering the health practices and medical care of the time. Six lived into their eighties, ten into their seventies, eleven into their sixties, seven into their fifties, five into their forties, four into their thirties, and three only into their twenties. Killed in action in 1864, Stephen Dodson Ramseur was the youngest to die, at age twenty-seven. William Ruffin Cox and Richard Caswell Gatlin lived longest, both dying at age eighty-seven.

As a group, the generals were well educated, especially for their time and place. Thirty-nine attended a college or university. Of that number, eighteen enrolled in the U.S. Military Academy at West Point before the war. All who attended graduated from the academy except Louis Addison Armistead and William Whedbee Kirkland, who were expelled. Two other generals, Robert Frederick Hoke and Alfred Iverson, attended a military institute for at least one year—Hoke in Kentucky and Iverson in Alabama. The remaining five had some degree of local or private schooling. The University of North Carolina at Chapel Hill can claim thirteen alumni among the generals. Twenty-seven of the forty-six Tar Heel commanders had some prewar military experience and training, serving in the Second Seminole War (1835–42), in the Mexican-American War (1846–48), on the western frontier, at some other place, or in the state Militia. Eleven served in the Mexican-American War, either as regular members of the U.S. Army or as state volunteers. That conflict especially is considered to have provided significant combat experience for officers in both the North and South.

Although some of North Carolina's Confederate generals questioned the wisdom of secession and a war for Southern independence, none publicly denied the constitutional right of the slaveholding states to secede, whether they were rabid or reluctant secessionists. Nor did any of them, with the possible exceptions of William Dorsey Pender and James Johnston Pettigrew—who opposed reopening the international slave trade—publicly express any moral ambiguity about the legality of slavery or its benefits as a labor system. Of course, the decision to join the Confederate army gives ample evidence of where their sectional loyalties ultimately lay, especially among the former U.S. Army officers who resigned their commissions to become soldiers of the South. Some of North Carolina's generals rushed to the Confederate banner as soon as South Carolina and six other slaveholding states seceded and formed the provisional Confederate States of America in early 1861. Others delayed until Confederate artillery fired on Fort Sumter in Charleston Harbor in April and Lincoln called on the states still in the Union for troops to suppress the rebellion. A few waited until North Carolina called its second Secession Convention on May 20 and then left the Union.

Most of the Tar Heel generals of the Confederacy who survived the war had successful postwar careers, as planters, lawyers, businessmen, engineers, educators, corporate officers, government officials, and politicians in both the state and national governments. A number had been members of the North Carolina legislature or the U.S. Congress before the war, and some held those offices after the conflict. Two, Daniel Gould Fowle and Alfred Moore Scales, served as governors of North Carolina. Those who became active in politics embraced the Democratic Party (called the Conservative Party in early Reconstruction). Only Rufus Barringer, who had been a strong Unionist before the war, is known to have joined the Republican Party.

George Burgwyn Anderson

1831–1862
Brigadier General

George Burgwyn Anderson was born near Hillsborough on April 12, 1831. He entered the University of North Carolina at Chapel Hill at age sixteen and attended that institution for one year before receiving an appointment to the U.S. Military Academy at West Point. In 1852, he graduated from the academy, where he ranked ninth in a class of forty-two. As a second lieutenant in the U.S. dragoons, he was briefly assigned to California. He soon joined a regiment at Fort Chadbourne, Texas, and was promoted to first lieutenant in 1855. He

served with his regiment in Kansas during the prewar violence that erupted in that territory, and he participated in future Confederate general Albert Sidney Johnston's expedition (1858–60) against the Mormons in Utah. In 1859, Anderson received orders for recruiting duty in Louisville, Kentucky. He remained at that post after South Carolina and six other slaveholding states seceded and formed the Confederate States of America in early 1861. But when Confederate troops fired on Fort Sumter in April, he resigned his U.S. commission and returned to North Carolina, which seceded from the Union on May 20 and joined the new Confederacy.

Four days before his native state's secession, Anderson had received an appointment as colonel of the Fourth Regiment North Carolina State Troops, which formed at Camp Hill, near Garysburg in Northampton County. Anderson's regiment was mustered into Confederate service on June 28, 1861. In July, the regiment received orders to move to the vicinity of Richmond, Virginia. By August 9, all of its companies had arrived at Camp Pickens, near Manassas Junction, and were soon assigned to the garrison at the junction. Anderson commanded that post, where his troops drilled and performed picket and fatigue duties in the fall and winter of 1861–62.

The troops then joined other regiments in the Peninsula Campaign (March–July 1862). In that campaign, General Joseph E. Johnston originally led the Confederate forces opposing the Army of the Potomac, under General George B. McClellan. The Federals had landed on the coast of Virginia and were advancing toward the Confederate capital at Richmond along the peninsula between the York and James Rivers. Anderson's troops saw their first major action at the Battle of Seven Pines on May 31. During that engagement, he temporarily commanded a brigade in General D.H. Hill's division. As Anderson led an assault down the Williamsburg Road, the attack stalled until he seized the flag of the Twenty-seventh Georgia and personally led the brigade in the capture of the Federal breastworks. For his courage and leadership, he received promotion to brigadier general and permanent command of a brigade.

Johnston had been wounded at Seven Pines and was succeeded by General Robert E. Lee, who reorganized the Confederates defending Richmond into the Army of Northern Virginia. Lee launched a series of counterattacks known as the Seven Days Battles (June 25–July 1) to drive McClellan's army from eastern Virginia. At the Battle of Gaines Mill on June 27, Anderson led his troops in an assault on an enemy position in an entangling swamp. Historian Douglas Southall Freeman described the North Carolinian's composure in that action: "G.B. Anderson—tall, erect, composed—found Federal infantry in the maze, but at the word of command in his magnificent voice his men drove out the enemy."

The Confederates' Seven Days assaults resulted in the Army of the Potomac's withdrawal to a heavily fortified position on Malvern Hill. On July 1, Lee ordered an all-out attack on that position. It proved costly in the number of casualties among his soldiers and failed to dislodge the defenders. Anderson's brigade had a large number of men killed, wounded, or missing. The general himself was wounded in the hand and had to be carried from the field. But despite the heavy losses that his soldiers inflicted on Lee's army, McClellan evacuated his troops from the peninsula.

Following Malvern Hill, the Army of Northern Virginia defeated the U.S. Army of Virginia, commanded by General John Pope, at the Second Battle of Manassas (or Bull Run) on August 29–30, 1862. After that victory, Lee decided to invade Maryland, and Anderson recovered from his wound in time to lead his brigade at the Battle of Sharpsburg (or Antietam) in September. As that engagement developed, his troops fended off a strong Federal attack at South Mountain and then held the right of the Confederate line in the famed Bloody Lane. As the line collapsed, Anderson stood on a nearby knoll in an attempt to rally the fleeing troops, and a minié ball struck him in the ankle. He subsequently traveled to Raleigh to recover from the wound, which at first was not considered serious. But infection set in, and surgeons amputated his foot. Anderson never recovered and died on October 16. He was buried at Oakwood Cemetery in Raleigh. He was survived by his wife, Mildred Ewing Anderson, whom he had married in November 1859, as well as one of their two children.

Historians generally agree that Anderson showed considerable skill as a combat leader, and had he lived, his ability and reputation as a Confederate general would have grown. Freeman paid special tribute to him, declaring that

> he had displayed qualities of stout leadership, though he never had been given opportunity in independent command. All the physical excellencies coveted by soldiers were abundantly his—a handsome figure, fine horsemanship, a clear musical voice, a commanding presence. His discipline had seemed as mild as his blue-gray eyes, but it had been firm. In battle, as he rode calmly alert, with his golden beard flowing, he had inspired his fine regiments.

Louis Addison Armistead

1817–1863
Brigadier General

L ouis Addison Armistead was born in New Bern, North Carolina, the eldest of four sons and second of nine children of U.S. Army officer Walter Keith Armistead of Virginia and Elizabeth Stanly Armistead of North Carolina. His birth occurred while his mother was visiting her parents, Congressman John Stanly and Elizabeth Frank Stanly. Armistead lived with his maternal grandparents for a year and then returned to his family on a three-acre farm in Fauquier County, Virginia.

Following the example of his father and four uncles, who fought in the War of 1812, Armistead sought a military career. He entered the U.S. Military Academy at West Point in 1834 but was expelled two years later for striking fellow cadet and future Confederate general Jubal A. Early on the head with a mess hall plate. Reportedly, Armistead felt that he had been "insulted" by Early.

Still desiring an army career, Armistead obtained a commission as a second lieutenant in the Sixth Regiment U.S. Infantry in 1839. He saw active duty in the Second Seminole War (1835–42). In 1844, he received promotion to first lieutenant. During the Mexican-American War (1846–48), he earned a reputation for courage and aggressive leadership in battle. For his performance, he was brevetted captain on August 20, 1847, and major on September 8, 1847. He was wounded at Chapultepec on September 13.

Following the Mexican-American War, Armistead served fourteen years on the western frontier and received promotion to captain in 1855. While at Fort Towson in present-day Oklahoma, he became good friends with future Union army general Winfield Scott Hancock of Pennsylvania. The two would later oppose each other on the battlefield at Gettysburg.

During the crisis that led to secession, Armistead remained committed to the Union. In the summer of 1860, he told a friend, "I know but one country and one flag." But as with so many of the Confederate generals who were serving in the U.S. Army at the outbreak of the Civil War, the firing on Fort Sumter and Lincoln's call for troops to suppress the rebellion led him to abandon his loyalty to the United States and become a soldier of the South. He resigned his commission in May 1861 and traveled back to the East from his station in Texas to offer his service to the Confederacy. At Richmond, he received a commission as colonel of the Fifty-seventh Regiment Virginia Infantry.

Armistead and his regiment served in western Virginia until his appointment in April 1862 as brigadier general in the division of Major General Benjamin Huger, who was in charge of the Norfolk District. Armistead's new command included five Virginia regiments. Huger's division abandoned the Norfolk area in the following month to participate in the defense against the advance of the Army of the Potomac, led by General George B. McClellan, toward Richmond along the peninsula between the York and James Rivers. During the Peninsula Campaign (March–July), the Confederate army opposing McClellan's force was originally commanded by General Joseph E. Johnston, who was wounded at the Battle of Seven Pines on May 31. General Robert E. Lee succeeded him and reorganized the Confederates into the Army of Northern Virginia. Lee ordered a series of counterattacks known as the Seven Days Battles (June 25–July 1) to drive the Federals from the peninsula. Armistead demonstrated courage, judgment, and leadership at the Battle of Seven Pines and at the Battle of Malvern Hill on July 1.

As the repulsed McClellan withdrew his forces from the peninsula, the Army of Northern Virginia defeated the U.S. Army of Virginia, commanded by General John Pope, at the Second Battle of Manassas (August 29–30). By the end of that battle, Armistead's reputation as a competent and courageous commander had been secured. One officer described him as "displaying everywhere conspicuous gallantry and winning by his coolness under fire, by his stern perseverance and his indomitable pluck, the applause of his superiors and the entire confidence of his men."

Following his success at Manassas, Lee appointed Armistead as his provost marshal general and marched his army into Maryland, where he clashed with McClellan's force at the Battle of Sharpsburg (or Antietam) on September 17. Armistead was wounded that day and temporarily left his brigade to recover.

Armistead had returned to his post by early December. In the meantime, his brigade had been transferred to the division of General George E. Pickett. Armistead's troops played only a minor role in Lee's victory at the Battle of Fredericksburg on December 13 and were under the command of General James Longstreet at Suffolk when the Battle of Chancellorsville occurred in May 1863.

But the general and his troops were to earn immortality at the Battle of Gettysburg (July 1–3). Following his victories at Fredericksburg and Chancellorsville, Lee invaded Pennsylvania and clashed with the Army of the Potomac, then commanded by General George G. Meade, at Gettysburg. On the third day of the battle, Armistead's brigade took part in the famed Pickett-Pettigrew assault on the strongly defended Federal center on Cemetery Ridge. During the attack, withering fire from the Union troops devastated the Confederate ranks. Armistead's horse was shot from under him. Then afoot, he placed his hat on his sword and called for his remaining men to "follow me." About one hundred of his troops reached the ridge and engaged in hand-to-hand combat with the Federals but failed to win the ground. After scaling the wall on the ridge, Armistead was hit in the chest and arm. Nevertheless, he staggered on until he reached a Union battery, where he fell mortally wounded. With their failed attack on Cemetery Ridge, the Confederates lost the Battle of Gettysburg.

When the remnants of the Confederate line retreated from Cemetery Ridge, the U.S. troops carried Armistead to the Eleventh Corps hospital at the George Spangler farm near the battlefield. Having sustained three wounds, he died on July 5. One of the many ironies of the Civil War was that his attack on Cemetery Ridge had been against troops commanded by a good friend from his prewar days, Winfield Scott Hancock. Armistead's body was buried in a temporary grave near the Spangler house but was soon removed and placed in the Hughes-Armistead vault at the St. Paul's Church cemetery in Baltimore, Maryland. Today, a monument stands at the point where Armistead's brigade penetrated the center of the Federal line. The site is known as the "high water mark of the Confederacy."

Armistead had twice become a widower. In February 1844, he married Cecelia Lee Love of Fairfax County, Virginia. They had two children, a daughter and a son, who for a time was his father's aide during the war. The daughter died in April 1850, and Cecelia died in December of that year. For a while, Armistead cared for his son on his own, but in March 1853, he married Cornelia L. Taliaferro Jameson, a naval officer's widow with a daughter, in Alexandria, Virginia. They subsequently had a son who died young. Cornelia died in August 1855.

Laurence Simmons Baker

1830–1907
Brigadier General

Laurence Simmons Baker was born at Coles Hill in Gates County on May 15, 1830. He received his early education in the county and at Norfolk Academy in Virginia. He graduated from the U.S. Military Academy at West Point in 1851. Commissioned a second lieutenant, he joined the Third U.S. Cavalry and served on the frontier, eventually attaining the rank of captain.

Baker originally opposed secession. Nevertheless, he resigned his U.S. commission four days after the North Carolina Secession Convention of May 20, 1861, withdrew the Tar Heel State from the Union. He then received a Confederate commission as a lieutenant colonel of cavalry and became second in command of the Ninth Regiment North Carolina State Troops (First Regiment North Carolina Cavalry) when that unit was organized at Camp Beauregard, near Ridgeway in Warren County, in August. Colonel Robert Ransom Jr. commanded the regiment, which in October transferred to Richmond and then to Manassas Junction, Virginia, where it joined the cavalry brigade of General J.E.B. Stuart.

Both Baker and Ransom were known for their commitment to drill and strict discipline. One of their soldiers said of them: "Their strict discipline aroused some bitter feeling on the part of both officers and men at first, but we soon found that they were right and that it was for our good."

The regiment participated in a number of operations in Virginia, mainly scouting and guard duty. On March 1, 1862, Ransom was promoted to brigadier general and transferred to command an infantry brigade. Baker replaced him as colonel of the regiment. Later that month, the Ninth was ordered back to North Carolina to help meet a Federal threat in the eastern part of the state. A Union expedition commanded by General Ambrose E. Burnside recently had captured Roanoke Island and soon took New Bern and control of much of the coastal area of the state. But in June, most of Baker's regiment was transferred back to Virginia to defend Richmond against the advance of the Army of the Potomac, led by General George B. McClellan, via the peninsula between the York and James Rivers.

In the Peninsula Campaign (March–July), General Joseph E. Johnston originally commanded the Confederate army opposing McClellan. Johnston, however, was wounded at the Battle of Seven Pines on May 31, and General Robert E. Lee took his place, reorganizing the Confederate troops in Virginia into the Army of Northern Virginia. Lee launched a series of counterattacks known as the Seven Days Battles (June 25–July 1) to drive the Federals from the peninsula. That operation culminated in the Battle of Malvern Hill on July 1, during which the Confederates suffered high casualties. Nevertheless, McClellan soon withdrew his army from eastern Virginia.

Baker's troops fought in the Seven Days Battles. When Stuart was promoted to major general to command a division (later a corps), Baker's regiment was assigned to the brigade of General Wade Hampton. The regiment guarded the Confederate capital at Richmond during the Second Battle of Manassas (August 29–30), where the Army of Northern Virginia defeated the U.S. Army of Virginia, commanded by General John Pope.

Following his success at Manassas, Lee decided to invade Maryland. At the ensuing Battle of Sharpsburg (or Antietam), his army was repulsed by McClellan's Army of the Potomac and was forced to retreat into Virginia. During the fighting, Baker's troops took part in cavalry operations. They were also at the Battle of Fredericksburg in December 1862, where Lee's soldiers inflicted a defeat and high casualties on the Army of the Potomac, then commanded by Burnside. At the Battle of Chancellorsville (May 1–3, 1863), where the Army of Northern Virginia scored another victory over the Army of the Potomac (commanded this time by General Joseph

Hooker), Hampton's brigade was on recruiting duty south of the James River. The Ninth Regiment (First Cavalry) saw action against Hooker's troops on June 9 at the Battle of Brandy Station, the largest cavalry operation of the war.

Building on his outcomes in Virginia, Lee decided to invade Pennsylvania in late June. During the ensuing Battle of Gettysburg (July 1–3), the Army of Northern Virginia was defeated by the Army of the Potomac, led then by General George G. Meade. Hampton was wounded on July 3, and Baker assumed command of the brigade. On that day, the Confederates' ill-conceived charge on the heavily fortified Union position at Cemetery Ridge proved disastrous for them. As Lee's devastated troops withdrew into Virginia, Baker's cavalrymen effectively covered the rear of the retreating army.

Having taken up a position along the Rappahannock River, Baker's troops repulsed an attack by Federal cavalry near Brandy Station in late July 1863. Stuart praised the North Carolinian's performance: "Hampton's brigade…was skillfully handled by Colonel Baker." Lee personally recommended Baker for promotion. Baker received his promotion and command of a new brigade of Tar Heel cavalrymen. Unfortunately, he had been wounded in the recent action at Brandy Station. The bones of his right arm had been shattered, and he underwent two operations in Richmond before going on a convalescent furlough. Unable to return to field service, he turned over command of his new brigade to General James B. Gordon.

As commander of the cavalry corps for the Army of Northern Virginia following the death of Stuart in May 1864, Hampton requested that Baker be promoted to major general and given command of a division. But his wound prevented Baker from accepting the assignment. Instead, he became commander of the Second Military District in North Carolina, with headquarters at Goldsboro and the mission of defending against Federal raids from the coast. He received another wound in a skirmish in September.

As the war drew toward its final months, Baker commanded a brigade of South Carolina Reserves against the U.S. campaign of General William T. Sherman in Georgia. Summoned back to North Carolina, he then led the First Brigade of Junior Reserves, boys seventeen years old, at the Battle of Bentonville in March 1865. That action was a final and failed attempt by the Confederate army commanded by Joseph E. Johnston to halt Sherman's advance. Detached after the battle from Johnston's main force to guard the Wilmington and Weldon Railroad, Baker and his troops surrendered upon hearing of Lee's surrender at Appomattox on April 9 and Johnston's later surrender to Sherman at Durham Station.

After the war, Baker lived and farmed near New Bern before engaging in a hauling business in Norfolk, Virginia, and then returning to North Carolina to work in insurance. In the late 1870s, he moved to Suffolk, Virginia, to accept a position with the Seaboard Airline Railway. He died there on April 10, 1907, and was buried at Cedar Hill Cemetery. In 1855, he married Elizabeth E. Henderson of Salisbury, and they had three children.

Rufus Barringer

1821–1895
Brigadier General

Rufus Barringer was born at Poplar Grove in Cabarrus County. His formal education began at Sugar Creek Academy in Mecklenburg County and continued at the University of North Carolina at Chapel Hill, from which he graduated in 1842. He studied law first in Concord, the seat of Cabarrus County, with his eldest brother, Daniel Moreau Barringer, a U.S. congressman and minister to Spain. He then continued his law studies with the well-known jurist Richmond Mumford Pearson, who later became chief justice of the North Carolina Supreme Court.

Admitted to the bar, Barringer began practicing law in his home county and soon entered state politics as a Whig. Elected to the House of Commons in 1848, he played an important role in the incorporation of the North Carolina Railroad Company. He served in the state Senate in 1850–51 and then returned to the practice of law in Cabarrus County. In 1854, he married Eugenia Morrison, daughter of the Reverend Robert Hall Morrison, the first president of Davidson College. Two of Morrison's other seven daughters also married Confederate generals. Isabella Sophia Morrison married D.H. Hill, and Mary Anna Morrison wed Thomas J. (Stonewall) Jackson.

Amid the bitter sectional discord tearing the nation apart in the 1850s, Barringer remained a staunch Unionist and opposed secession. During the presidential election of 1860, he served as an elector for John Bell, the candidate of the Constitutional Union Party. That party included many former Whigs, opposed secession, and called for the states to stand by the Union and the U.S. Constitution. But after Confederates fired on Fort Sumter in April 1861 and President Lincoln called for troops to suppress the rebellion, Barringer believed that the secession of his state was inevitable, and he began to prepare for war by raising a company of state troops for possible Confederate service. In late May, North Carolina seceded from the Union and joined the Confederate States of America.

Captain Barringer's unit became Company F of the Ninth Regiment North Carolina State Troops (First Regiment North Carolina Cavalry) when it was organized at Camp Beauregard in Warren County in August 1861. Colonel Robert Ransom Jr. commanded the regiment, which transferred in October to Richmond and then to Manassas Junction in Virginia, as a component of General J.E.B. Stuart's cavalry. The regiment performed mainly scouting and guard duty until it was ordered back to North Carolina in March 1862 to meet a possible Federal attack in the eastern part of the state. A Federal expedition led by General Ambrose E. Burnside had recently captured Roanoke Island and New Bern and controlled a number of coastal counties, posing a threat to the interior of the state.

Barringer's company returned to Virginia to aid in repulsing General George B. McClellan's Army of the Potomac advancing on Richmond along the peninsula between the York and James Rivers. In the Peninsula Campaign (March–July 1862), General Joseph E. Johnston originally commanded the Confederate force opposing McClellan. But after he was wounded at the Battle of Seven Pines on May 31, General Robert E. Lee took his place and reorganized the Confederate troops into the Army of Northern Virginia. Lee then launched a series of counterattacks known as the Seven Days Battles (June 25–July 1) to drive the Federals from the peninsula. That operation ended on July 1 with the Battle of Malvern Hill, where a Confederate attack on a strongly fortified Union position produced heavy casualties among Lee's troops and failed to dislodge McClellan's men, who nonetheless would soon evacuate eastern Virginia.

After Malvern Hill, Lee divided his cavalry into two brigades under the command of General Stuart. The Ninth Regiment (First Cavalry) was assigned to Stuart's first brigade, commanded by General Wade Hampton of South Carolina. The regiment was left behind to guard Richmond during the Second Battle of Manassas (August 29–30, 1862), in which the Army of Northern Virginia defeated the U.S. Army of Virginia, commanded by General John Pope. Barringer's company took part in an action at White Oak Swamp as McClellan's troops retreated from the peninsula. The Ninth then rejoined the rest of Lee's army on September 2 in time for its invasion of Maryland. Barringer's Company F did not participate in the subsequent Battle of Sharpsburg (or Antietam) on September 17, but it did engage in skirmishes as the Confederate cavalry reconnoitered the Federals and screened Lee's retreating column. McClellan's Army of the Potomac had repulsed the Army of Northern Virginia and forced its withdrawal across the Potomac River.

During the Confederate victory at the Battle of Fredericksburg in December, Barringer's regiment attacked the supply lines of Burnside, who had replaced McClellan in command of the Army of the Potomac. At Fredericksburg, Burnside ordered a disastrous charge against the heavily fortified Confederate position on Marye's Heights. Because of his loss at Fredericksburg, he was replaced by General Joseph Hooker.

Lee defeated Hooker at the Battle of Chancellorsville in May 1863, but during the decisive Confederate victory, Hampton's brigade was "south of the James River recruiting." It then assembled with other units of the Army of Northern Virginia at Culpeper Court House for an anticipated campaign. At the Battle of Brandy Station on June 9, Barringer's regiment fought for most of the day and at one point routed the Tenth Regiment New York Cavalry, capturing its standard. During the fighting, Barringer received a severe wound to his face, but according to General Hampton, he "bore himself with marked coolness and good conduct." A minié ball struck him in the right cheek, passing into his mouth and fracturing the superior maxilla and dislocating the upper teeth. Surgeons tended the wound the same day, but the injury remained permanent. Barringer was hospitalized in Salisbury, North Carolina, and remained on medical leave through August, missing the famed Battle of Gettysburg (July 1–3).

Upon returning to duty in Virginia, Barringer was promoted to major and transferred from Company F to the field and staff of the Ninth Regiment (First Cavalry). Other changes also took place in his brigade. Colonel Laurence S. Baker was elevated to brigadier general and command of what had been Hampton's brigade. Hampton became the commander of one of the divisions of the newly organized cavalry corps of General Stuart, and when General Baker was given special duty because of wounds, Colonel James B. Gordon rose to command the brigade in Hampton's new division.

In early October, Lee crossed the Rappahannock River and engaged the Army of the Potomac, commanded by General George G. Meade, in an action that came to be known as the Bristoe Campaign, which lasted until October 20, when Lee's army withdrew across the Rappahannock. During the operation, Barringer and his fellow cavalrymen were engaged at Russell's Ford, James City, Culpeper Court House, and Auburn Mills. At the latter site, on October 14, Colonel Thomas Ruffin, who had replaced Gordon as regimental commander, led a charge against infantry skirmishes threatening Confederate artillery. After Ruffin was wounded, Barringer quickly rallied the regiment and led another charge that forced the enemy to flee.

Although slightly wounded at Auburn Mills, Barringer remained on duty and, on October 19, led his regiment in a drastic charge at Buckland Mills, near Warrenton, Virginia. Frequently referred to as the Buckland Races, the attack completely routed a detachment of Union cavalry, who "fled in great confusion and were pursued for several miles with unrelenting fury." Stuart sent Barringer a complimentary letter in which he referred to the North Carolinian's command "as a pattern for others." He soon received promotion to lieutenant colonel. William H. Cheek was promoted from lieutenant colonel to full colonel and given command of the regiment. In the ensuing Mine Run Campaign below the Rapidan River, Lee managed to force Meade's withdrawal across the river. During the operation, the Ninth Regiment served as support for artillery and dismounted troops and engaged in some skirmishing. Both armies then went into winter quarters.

On January 1, 1864, Barringer left the Ninth Regiment to assume temporary command of the Fifty-ninth Regiment North Carolina Troops (Fourth Regiment North Carolina Cavalry). That unit traveled to eastern North Carolina for recruiting and picketing duty and in May was assigned to the District of Petersburg, Virginia, where it took part in operations in the Richmond vicinity.

In the meantime, General Ulysses S. Grant had become general in chief of the Union army, taken personal command of the Army of the Potomac, with Meade as a subordinate, and launched his Overland Campaign (May–June 1864). Grant's objectives were to keep constant pressure on Lee's army, force it back toward Richmond, and eventually effect its surrender. The Federals had heavy losses at the Battles of the Wilderness (May 5–6), Spotsylvania Court House (May 7–19), and Cold Harbor (June 1–3), but they ultimately forced the Army of Northern Virginia into trenches at Petersburg. At about the same time, the Army of Northern Virginia transferred its North Carolina cavalry brigade from Hampton's division to the division of General William Henry Fitzhugh Lee, where it remained for the rest of the war. Before and during the Battle of the Wilderness, the brigade rendered important service in helping to check Grant's advance, reporting hostile movements, protecting the infantry, and taking prisoners.

When General Philip H. Sheridan and twelve thousand Yankee horsemen launched a raid toward Richmond on May 9, Gordon's brigade undertook to thwart their progress and, in the fighting that followed, lost soldiers and horses. With his other brigades, Stuart managed to get in front of and halt the Federal advance. But the dashing Confederate cavalry commander fell mortally wounded at Yellow Tavern. Gordon also received a wound on May 12 and soon died.

Barringer continued to lead the Fifty-ninth Regiment (Fourth Cavalry) until Gordon's death. Then the North Carolinian returned to his old regiment, the Ninth (First Cavalry), and soon took command of the deceased Gordon's Tar Heel brigade, with the date of rank of brigadier general from June 1. As part of the Army of Northern Virginia's cavalry corps, newly commanded by Hampton since the death of Stuart, Barringer and his North Carolinians participated in numerous engagements leading up to and including the Battle of Cold Harbor.

With the main body of Lee's army entrenched, Barringer's brigade performed a number of raids and operations in the Petersburg area, including preventing Union troops from cutting or controlling the Petersburg and Weldon Railroad and the Richmond and Danville Railroad. At Reams's Station on August 25, 1864, a combined attack of Confederate infantry, artillery, and cavalry finally drove the Federals from the Petersburg and Weldon Railroad. During that engagement, General William H.F. Lee was absent because of illness, and command of his division fell to Barringer. The cavalry attacked the Federals in their front, while the infantry and artillery assailed them in the rear. General Robert E. Lee subsequently remarked that "the brigade of Genl. Barringer bore a conspicuous part in the operations of the cavalry."

After Reams's Station, Barringer's brigade participated in "eight severe actions" in the vicinity and "fought with varied success" in the famed Hampton's Beefsteak Raid, in which the Confederate cavalry halted a stampede and secured a large herd of cattle for Lee's starving troops. After the raid, Barringer's men took part in a number of further actions to protect the Petersburg and Weldon Railroad before going into winter quarters near Belfield, where they rested, recruited, and performed picket duty.

At the Battle of Five Forks on March 31–April 1, 1865, Barringer's troops attempted to halt U.S. cavalry led by General Philip H. Sheridan, but they were forced to move to Namozine Church, having heard that the Army of Northern Virginia had finally abandoned its trenches and was fleeing westward. At Namozine Church on April 3, Barringer's soldiers took a position to await the attack of the Federal cavalry. In the ensuing battle, the brigade was virtually destroyed. "With less than eight hundred men in the line," Barringer later wrote, "I had to receive the shock of over eight thousand," along with an order "to fight to the last." He was captured by a small party of U.S. scouts shortly after the battle. He therefore was not with the remnants of his brigade when they joined the rest of the Army of Northern Virginia as it fled westward. Lee finally surrendered that army to Grant at Appomattox Court House on April 9.

Barringer was transferred to City Point, Virginia, and placed under guard. While there, he met President Abraham Lincoln. Lincoln had gone to City Point to confer with General Grant, who had established his center of operations there. Accounts of the meeting between the Confederate general and the U.S. chief executive vary, but apparently a Federal officer at the site where a number of captured Confederate officers were housed in tents introduced Barringer to the president. Lincoln at first might have confused Barringer with his brother, Daniel Moreau Barringer, a congressman whom Lincoln claimed had sat with him before the war in the "Cherokee Strip," an overflow of Whigs across the main aisle in the U.S. House of Representatives.

In the course of the conversation between Lincoln and Barringer, the general asked if he might be sent to the U.S. prison at Fort Delaware rather than the one at Johnson's Island, Ohio. He had friends in nearby Philadelphia, he said, who might visit or otherwise be of service to him. Lincoln wrote a note, perhaps on the back of an official card, authorizing Barringer's request and handed it to the general.

The Federals then transferred Barringer to Old Capitol Prison in Washington, D.C. While he was there, Lincoln was assassinated on April 14, and a week later, Barringer requested to see Secretary of War Edwin M. Stanton. At the subsequent meeting, the general presented Lincoln's note to Stanton and requested to be moved to Fort Delaware. Stanton questioned Barringer at length, possibly in part to determine if he had any knowledge of the events leading to the assassination. The secretary of war then assigned Barringer to Fort Delaware. He was released from prison on July 25, arriving home on August 8.

Barringer moved to Charlotte and again took up his practice of law. He joined the Republican Party and supported Congressional Reconstruction, although he was not generally referred to as a "scalawag," a term often applied by white southerners to native sons who joined the Republican Party and supported its Reconstruction policies. He served as a member of the state Constitutional Convention of 1875 and ran unsuccessfully as the Republican candidate for lieutenant governor in 1880. He retired from the bar in 1884 and devoted himself to writing about his wartime experiences. He supported temperance reform and industrial education and served as a trustee of the North Carolina College of Agriculture and Mechanic Arts (now North Carolina State University) in Raleigh, chartered in 1887.

In the spring of 1894, Barringer's health began to decline, and he sought recovery in northern sanitariums. But he soon accepted that he was not going to live long and returned home to Charlotte, where he died of stomach cancer on February 3, 1895. He was buried in Elmwood Cemetery in that city.

Barringer married three times. His first wife, Eugenia, died in 1858, and in 1861 he married Rosalie Chunn of Charlotte. After her death, he married Margaret Long of Orange County. He had three sons, one with each of his wives.

John Decatur Barry

1839–1867
Brigadier General (Temporary)

John Decatur Barry was born in Wilmington, North Carolina, and attended the University of North Carolina from 1856 to 1859. He resided as a banker in Wilmington until August 1861, when he enlisted as a private in Company I, known as the Wilmington Rifle Guards, of the Eighth Regiment North Carolina Volunteers, which transferred from state service to Confederate service around that time. In November, the regiment deployed for service in South Carolina, where its name changed to the Eighteenth Regiment North Carolina Troops.

When a large portion of coastal North Carolina and the town of New Bern fell to a Federal expedition led by General Ambrose E. Burnside in March 1862, the regiment relocated to Kinston, North Carolina, where it became part of the brigade commanded by General Lawrence O'Bryan Branch. On April 24, Barry was elected captain of Company I. At the same time, Robert H. Cowan replaced James D. Radcliffe as colonel of the regiment. In November 1862, Colonel Thomas J. Purdie replaced Cowan, and he led the regiment until his death at Chancellorsville, Virginia, in May 1863.

In early May 1862, Branch's brigade was ordered to Virginia, where a Federal force under the command of General George B. McClellan was advancing toward Richmond from the east via the peninsula between the James and York Rivers. General Joseph E. Johnston commanded the Confederate army opposing McClellan in the Peninsula Campaign (March–July 1862). During that campaign, Barry saw his first major action at Hanover Court House on May 27. Three days later, General Johnston was wounded, and Robert E. Lee became commander of the Confederate troops in Virginia. Lee soon organized them into the Army of Northern Virginia and then launched a counterattack on McClellan known as the Seven Days Battles (June 25– July 1). During that fighting, Barry was wounded at the Battle of Frayser's Farm (also called White Oak Swamp) on June 30. He remained absent from duty until probably sometime in October. On November 11, 1862, he was promoted to major and transferred to the regiment's field and staff.

Barry and his troops went into action on the evening of the first day of the Battle of Chancellorsville in May 1863, when Lee's army clashed with the Army of the Potomac, then led by General Joseph Hooker. The Eighteenth sustained a large number of casualties, with thirty-four killed, ninety-nine wounded, and twenty-one missing. Colonel Purdie was killed and his second in command wounded. In fact, all thirteen field officers in the Eighteenth Regiment became casualties, except Barry. He then received a promotion to colonel and command of the regiment.

Although the Army of Northern Virginia drove Hooker's force from the field on May 3 and won a major victory at Chancellorsville, it suffered a serious blow when General Thomas J. (Stonewall) Jackson was killed by fire from his own troops. Apparently, Barry himself ordered the volley that felled Jackson. In the late afternoon of May 2, Jackson, whose brilliant flanking of Hooker's army helped carry the battle for the Confederates, rode out with his staff to make a reconnaissance of the enemy's position. When Jackson and his staff returned through thick woods to their own lines, Barry's regiment mistook them for Union soldiers and opened fire. Jackson was mortally wounded, and Barry took responsibility and blamed himself for ordering the volley that killed the famed general.

After his success at Chancellorsville, Lee marched his army into Pennsylvania, where in the first week of July he fought the Battle of Gettysburg against the Army of the Potomac, then commanded by General George G. Meade. During the vicious fighting, Barry led the Eighteenth North Carolina in the Confederates' ill-fated charge up the famed Cemetery Ridge. One of his soldiers later described the attack:

Suddenly the enemy's artillery ceased and we were ordered forward to charge the heights occupied by the enemy's artillery and infantry. We faced the storm of death-dealing grape, shell and canister shot, and an incessant shower of musketry, a long distance in an open field, all the way, and reaching the heights only to find that we were flanked by the enemy and unsupported by our own troops, we were compelled to fall back, leaving many of our best and brave men dead and dying on this bloody and sanguinary field.

Soundly defeated at Gettysburg, Lee withdrew his army into Virginia.

Barry remained at the head of his troops during the subsequent and bloody Battles of the Wilderness and Spotsylvania Court House in Virginia in May 1864. Those battles were the result of a plan by General Ulysses S. Grant, the new general in chief of the Union armies, to attack and keep relentless pressure on the Army of Northern Virginia, driving it back toward Richmond and forcing its surrender. To carry out his Overland Campaign (May–June), Grant personally took charge of the Army of the Potomac, under the direct command of Meade. At the Wilderness and Spotsylvania battles, Grant paid a terrible price in soldiers killed and wounded.

At the Battle of Cold Harbor (June 1–3), in which the Army of the Potomac again suffered horrendous losses, Barry took command of his entire brigade when General James Henry Lane, who had replaced Branch, was wounded by a sharpshooter. After Cold Harbor, Grant flanked Lee's army and attacked Petersburg, south of Richmond. There the two armies became entrenched in a siege that lasted virtually until Lee's surrender at Appomattox Court House in April 1865. During the siege, however, Barry's brigade "was not kept in the trenches, but was a 'flying infantry' or 'foot cavalry.'" Lane praised Barry's leadership in his absence.

It was during such "flying infantry" operations that Barry was wounded yet again. "Whilst on a reconnoitering tour on or about July 2, 1864," the young acting brigadier was struck in the right hand by a ball from a sharpshooter. Surgeons amputated his second and third fingers. On August 8, Barry received official appointment as temporary brigadier general, dating from August 3. But his wound had so impaired him that he remained absent from duty until January or February 1865.

In the meantime, Lane resumed command of the brigade, which saw action in a number of hostile encounters in the Petersburg vicinity. Barry therefore lost his temporary rank as brigadier general. Although he returned to command the Eighteenth Regiment as a colonel, his wound incapacitated him to the extent that a board of surgeons recommended that he be retired from active field service. He left the regiment in March 1865 to assume departmental duty in North Carolina and served in his native state until the end of the war, when he was paroled in Raleigh on May 12.

Following the war, Barry's health deteriorated progressively. He returned to Wilmington and, in partnership with William H. Bernard, established the *Wilmington Dispatch*, a leading Conservative (or Democratic) Party newspaper, which published its first issue on October 1, 1865. The partnership quickly dissolved, but Barry continued producing the *Dispatch* for a while. Bad health continued to plague him, however, and he died at his mother's house in Wilmington in March 1867. He was buried at that city's Oakdale Cemetery. In 1863, Barry had married Fannie Jones of Hampton, Virginia, who survived him. One officer who served with Barry later called him "as gallant a soldier as ever buckled on a sword."

Braxton Bragg

1817–1876
Full General

B raxton Bragg was born in Warrenton, North Carolina, on March 22, 1817. He attended Warrenton Academy and then the U.S. Military Academy at West Point, where he graduated near the top of his class in 1837. He served in Florida's Second Seminole War (1835–42). When his health failed, he returned home to recover before resuming duty. Showing a quarrelsome and critical nature that persisted and marred his entire military career, Bragg received official reprimands and a temporary suspension of rank and command for publicly criticizing the policies of the army and its commander, General Winfield Scott.

During the Mexican-American War (1846–48), Bragg performed admirably as an officer of artillery, being twice brevetted and then promoted permanently to captain. He subsequently served at New Orleans and at various posts on the frontier, a duty that he disdained. Quarreling with Secretary of War Jefferson Davis over his assignment, he resigned his commission in December 1855 and the following February purchased a sugar plantation in Louisiana. He had success as a planter as well as a commissioner of public works, designing and building drainage and levee systems. As the sectional dispute over slavery and its extension led toward separation and war, he originally disapproved of secession, but eventually he accepted it as inevitable in the face of the growing bitterness between North and South and between slaveholders and antislavery advocates.

When Louisiana seceded in January 1861, the governor appointed Bragg a major general and placed him in charge of the state's forces. Then President Jefferson Davis made him a brigadier general in the Confederate army in March, and the War Department ordered him to Pensacola, Florida, to train volunteers. About six months later, Bragg received a promotion to major general and command of western Florida and all of Alabama.

In February 1862, he transferred to the western army of General Albert Sidney Johnston in northern Mississippi. There Bragg took command of Johnston's Second Corps and simultaneously served as chief of staff. He held those responsibilities during the Battle of Pittsburg Landing (or Shiloh), where, in early 1862, Johnston's army attacked the Federal force of General Ulysses S. Grant. Bragg commanded troops near the center of the battlefield. The Federals won the battle, in which Johnston was killed, and General Pierre G.T. Beauregard assumed command of the western army.

On April 12, President Davis appointed Bragg a full general. The president then assigned him command of the Western Department when Beauregard decided to take a leave of absence. In August, Bragg began an invasion of the border state of Kentucky (which remained in the Union throughout the war), but in October he was repulsed by the forces of General Don Carlos Buell at the Battle of Perryville and forced to retreat into Tennessee. In November, the Confederacy's Army of Tennessee was formed as the principal army of the west under Bragg. He next faced General William S. Rosecrans at the Battle of Murfreesboro, which began on December 31. Two days later, a final attack by Bragg failed, and he withdrew from Murfreesboro to Chattanooga, where he continued to joust with Rosecrans.

The two finally did full battle at Chickamauga Creek on September 19 and 20. With the arrival from Virginia of reinforcements commanded by General James Longstreet and the timeliness of a Confederate attack, Bragg's force drove the Federals from the field. Bragg then moved his troops to the heights around Chattanooga, facing Rosecrans. As these events unfolded, Bragg persisted in quarreling with his subordinates and missed a number of opportunities to follow up on his victory at Chickamauga.

As he hesitated, the U.S. War Department replaced Rosecrans with the more aggressive Grant, who on September 24 and 25 drove the Confederates off Lookout Mountain and Missionary Ridge, forcing their retreat into

Georgia. After condemning and blaming his subordinates for the defeat, Bragg requested to be relieved of his western command. President Davis quickly accepted the resignation and called Bragg to Richmond to serve as his military adviser. While functioning as Davis's chief of staff, Bragg performed well in a number of instances. He eliminated corruption in the Conscription Bureau and gave Davis some good advice regarding military affairs. The president, however, did not always listen to Bragg, and the two stubborn and opinionated men frequently disagreed.

In October 1864, although still serving as military adviser to Davis, Bragg transferred to Wilmington, North Carolina, the Confederacy's last effective blockade-running port. At that post, he displayed only incompetence. When, in January 1865, the Federals attacked Fort Fisher, which guarded Wilmington, to close the port, Bragg refused to release troops in the town to help defend the fortification. He merely stood by and let the fort and town fall. His excuses for this behavior were flimsy and illogical.

When General William T. Sherman invaded North Carolina in the last months of the war, Bragg served as a division commander under General Joseph E. Johnston, then commanding the remnants of the Army of Tennessee defending against Sherman's onslaught in the Carolinas. At Goldsboro and Wise's Forks, Bragg's division attempted to halt or slow a Federal advance from the coast but failed. Following Robert E. Lee's surrender to Grant at Appomattox Court House in Virginia in April, Johnston surrendered to Sherman at the Bennett Farmhouse, near Durham Station, North Carolina, thus effectively ending the Civil War.

When Davis and his cabinet fled south from Richmond in the final weeks of the war, Bragg joined them for a time. On May 10, 1865, near Concord, Georgia, U.S. Cavalry captured Bragg and his wife, the former Eliza Brooks Ellis of Louisiana, as they made their way home. He received a parole at that site. His postwar career included working as a civil engineer in Texas and Alabama. He died in Galveston, Texas, in 1876 and was buried in Mobile, Alabama.

Bragg had promise as a general but failed to fulfill it as a field commander. His greatest success came as adviser to the Confederate president. He lacked the capacity to inspire loyalty or confidence in his subordinate officers, who at one point officially called for his dismissal. His discipline of his troops was harsh and unreasonable, and he failed to admit his mistakes or learn from them. Bragg's large ego and defensive, rigid, and argumentative personality made it most difficult for others to cooperate with him. Nevertheless, he held the highest rank of all the North Carolina generals. The U.S. Army's Fort Bragg is named for him.

Lawrence O'Bryan Branch

1820–1862
Brigadier General

Lawrence O'Bryan Branch was born in Enfield, North Carolina, but spent his early childhood in Tennessee. After the death of his parents, he returned to North Carolina and joined the household of his prominent uncle John Branch, a legislator, governor of North Carolina, U.S. senator, secretary of the navy, and governor of Florida. When President Andrew Jackson appointed his uncle to the naval post, Branch accompanied his kinsman to Washington, D.C., where he studied with a number of tutors, including the influential politician and future U.S. secretary of the treasury and Supreme Court justice Salmon P. Chase. He then returned to the Tar Heel State to study at the Bingham School, an academy in Hillsborough. He attended the University of North Carolina before transferring to Princeton University, from which he graduated with distinction in 1838.

Branch worked as a newspaper editor in Tennessee while studying for the law. He relocated to Florida and in 1840 was admitted to the bar in that state, although because of his young age, a special act of the legislature was required for his admission. In the Second Seminole War (1835–42), he served as an aide to General Robert R. Reid. He then moved to Raleigh, North

Carolina, practiced law, and in 1852 became president of the Raleigh and Gaston Railroad. Becoming active in politics as a southern rights Democrat, he served in the U.S. House of Representatives from 1855 to 1861 and was a strong supporter of President James Buchanan, although he declined the cabinet posts of postmaster general and secretary of the treasury.

As the sectional crisis reached a crescendo, Branch advocated secession. Following North Carolina's withdrawal from the Union, he enlisted as a private in the Raleigh Rifles, but the governor soon appointed him state quartermaster general. He resigned that position to become colonel of the Thirty-third Regiment North Carolina Troops. In January 1862, he received promotion to brigadier general in the Confederate army. In that capacity, he commanded the defense of New Bern against the Federal attack led by General Ambrose E. Burnside in March. Burnside's victory at the coastal town followed his success at Roanoke Island in February. Having defeated Branch's force, the Federals established their headquarters at New Bern and controlled much of coastal North Carolina for the rest of the war. After the battle, Branch's forces retreated to Kinston. Although he commanded overall operations, Branch himself escaped much of the blame that officials and the public levied against other officers for the loss of New Bern, a serious blow to North Carolina. He was transferred to Virginia to command his brigade, which was then composed of the Seventh, Eighteenth, Twenty-eighth, Thirty-third, and Thirty-seventh Regiments North Carolina Troops.

During the subsequent Peninsula Campaign (March–July 1862), in which General George B. McClellan and the U.S. Army of the Potomac advanced from the coast toward Richmond along the peninsula between the York and James Rivers, Branch's brigade participated in the battle at Hanover Court House on May 27, 1862. There the Confederate troops were forced to withdraw, and Branch received no praise for his performance, although historian Douglas Southall Freeman concluded that the retreat was "in no sense discreditable to Branch." After General Joseph E. Johnston, commanding the Confederate army opposing McClellan, was wounded at the Battle of Seven Pines on May 31, General Robert E. Lee replaced him and reorganized the Confederate units into the Army of Northern Virginia.

At that time, Branch's brigade, which had been operating independently, became part of General A.P. Hill's Light Division. Branch and his troops took part in the ensuing Seven Days Battles (June 25–July 1), in which Lee struck McClellan hard and repeatedly in a number of bloody engagements to dislodge him from the peninsula. At the Battle of Frayser's Farm (or White

Oak Swamp) on June 30, a portion of Branch's brigade was overwhelmed and broke from the battle line. A.P. Hill himself rode forward, seized the flag of the Seventh Regiment, and called to the men as they ran to the rear, "Damn you, if you will not follow me, I will die alone." Stirred by Hill's courage, Branch's fleeing soldiers halted and regrouped. Lee's counterattack against McClellan on the peninsula ended at the Battle of Malvern Hill, during which Branch's troops were held in reserve.

Their next major action occurred at the Battle of Cedar Mountain on August 9. In that struggle, the Army of Northern Virginia clashed with the Federals' newly formed Army of Virginia, commanded by General John Pope. The Confederates achieved a hard-fought victory. Branch and his men performed well, but not, according to historian Robert K. Krick, "as well as he boasted in public and private writings." During that summer, Branch's health suffered when he developed bowel trouble. At Cedar Mountain, he was so incapacitated by the heat and diarrhea that he had to ride in an ambulance. Lee and Pope confronted each other again at the Second Battle of Manassas (or Bull Run) on August 29–30. As part of the Confederate victory, Branch's brigade helped to defend the left of the line.

When the Army of Northern Virginia invaded Maryland in mid-September, Branch's troops assisted in the capture of Harpers Ferry. At the Battle of Sharpsburg (or Antietam) on September 17, Branch was killed. Two versions exist for the circumstances of his death. One asserts that a sharpshooter's bullet struck him in the head while he conferred with A.P. Hill and two other brigadiers. Another account claims that he was killed while leading his troops. Branch's body was brought back to Raleigh, where he was buried at City Cemetery.

In 1844, Branch had married Nancy Haywood Blount of Washington, North Carolina. They had one surviving son.

David Clark

1820–1882
Brigadier General of Militia

D avid Clark was born on February 11, 1820, at Albin Plantation near Scotland Neck in Halifax County, North Carolina. His father was a wealthy planter, and Clark enjoyed the privileges of that class. He attended Raleigh's Episcopal School of North Carolina for Boys. He settled in Littleton and became a successful planter with several plantations and a large number of slaves, as well as a sizable library.

Clark's political views featured a strong endorsement of states' rights. In December 1861, the state's adjutant general, James G. Martin, ordered him, as colonel of the Fifteenth Regiment of Militia, to assist in organizing the northeast section of the state to meet a possible Union invasion. Clark obtained weapons and supplies from Raleigh and Norfolk and by early January had established a system of defense and early warning.

The anticipated Federal invasion of northeastern North Carolina came when a U.S. force commanded by General Ambrose E. Burnside captured Roanoke Island and moved onto the mainland to take over a number of towns and much of the coastal region, including New Bern, where the Northern army established its headquarters. The Federals would occupy much of coastal North Carolina for the rest of the war.

As Burnside threatened from Roanoke Island, a virtual panic set in among the populace of the northeastern counties. For defense, Governor Henry T. Clark (no relation to David Clark) ordered out the Militia, including the Fifteenth Regiment. David Clark directed the Militia in blocking the Roanoke River with four sunken vessels and a number of felled trees. The governor ordered him to maintain the protection and obstruction of the river, giving him the authority to impress supplies and equipment from the locals and to arrest anyone suspected of being disloyal to the Confederacy. Impressed with Clark's "executive ability, great energy and zeal for the cause," the state's chief executive promoted him to brigadier general and gave him command of seven Militia regiments. Clark continued to direct the Militia units in the area until April 1862, when Confederate troops relieved them. He then returned to managing his plantations, although still performing limited duty with the Militia.

After the war, Clark ran his plantations until his death on October 4, 1882, at Airlie Plantation in Halifax County. He was buried at the Thorne-Clark Cemetery near Bethel Hill. Clark was married to the former Anna Maria Thorne of Halifax County. Their son was Walter McKenzie Clark, the well-known Progressive, author, and chief justice of the state supreme court.

Thomas Lanier Clingman

1812–1897
Brigadier General

Thomas Lanier Clingman was born on
July 27, 1812, at Huntsville in Surry
(now Yadkin) County. After his merchant
father died, he was raised and educated
by his mother and an uncle. He graduated
from the University of North Carolina
at Chapel Hill at the head of his class in
1832. He read law in Hillsborough with the
prominent North Carolina political leader
William A. Graham and was admitted
to the bar. He was elected to the North
Carolina House of Commons from Surry
County in 1835 as a Whig, supporting
amendments to the state constitution.

Unsuccessful in reelection the next year, he moved to Asheville, in Buncombe
County, and practiced law.

In 1840, Clingman was elected to the state Senate, and three years later, he
was serving in the U.S. House of Representatives. Except for the term 1845–47,
he remained in that body until 1858, when he filled the unexpired term of Asa
Biggs in the U.S. Senate. He was elected to the Senate in his own right in 1860,
resigning in late March 1861 and calling for the secession of his native state.

Clingman was originally a die-hard Whig whose opposition to
the annexation of Texas and the gag rule, which opposed abolitionist

petitions in Congress, probably cost him the 1845–47 term in the House. His vehement attacks on Democrats led to a duel with Democrat and strong southern rights advocate William L. Yancey of Alabama. Fortunately, both combatants missed when they fired, and apologies reconciled the two. As the national dispute over slavery and its extension into the new territories grew, Clingman drifted away from the Whig Party, and by the time of the war, he had joined the secessionist Democrats to defend what he considered the interests and constitutional rights of the slaveholding states. He served for a short time as a delegate to the provisional government of the Confederacy in Montgomery, Alabama (which remained the Confederate capital until July 1862, when the seat of government moved to Richmond, Virginia).

Although he lacked military experience, Clingman received a commission as colonel of the Twenty-fifth Regiment North Carolina Troops in September 1861. He led that regiment in eastern North Carolina and Virginia until May 1862, when he received promotion to brigadier general. On August 7, he reported that he could not walk or ride a horse because his foot was inflamed. Eleven days later, he received orders to take charge of the defenses at Wilmington, North Carolina. In September, Clingman was on sick leave, and General Robert E. Lee, commanding the Confederate force in Virginia, declared that he should remain in North Carolina, where he would be more useful than in Virginia. Clingman then engaged in operations in coastal North and South Carolina, including a defense of Goldsboro. In a failed attempt by the Confederate force under General George Pickett to recapture New Bern from the Federals in February 1864, Clingman's troops formed in line when Union artillery fired on them, and Clingman was hit by several shell fragments. Only slightly wounded, he remained with his unit.

At the Battle of Drewry's Bluff in Virginia on May 16, 1864, Clingman's brigade saw action as part of General Robert F. Hoke's division. In overall command of the Confederate victory was General Pierre G.T. Beauregard, whose force defeated the U.S. force led by General Benjamin F. Butler. On May 31, Clingman's troops also took part in the Battle of Cold Harbor, where Lee's Army of Northern Virginia exacted a terrible toll from the Army of the Potomac, directly commanded by General George G. Meade and accompanied by the general in chief of the Union armies, Ulysses S. Grant. In that action, Clingman suffered a slight wound when a piece of shell tore the front of his hat and struck him in the forehead. Only temporarily stunned, he remained on the field. He continued to lead his troops in actions in the vicinity of Petersburg, where Grant's and Lee's armies became entrenched and stalemated, before Lee finally surrendered at Appomattox Court House on April 9, 1865.

At a battle along the Petersburg and Weldon Railroad on August 19, Clingman was severely wounded in the leg, and he was forced to convalesce in North Carolina. In the final weeks of the war, when General William T. Sherman entered North Carolina opposed by the remnants of the Confederacy's western army, commanded by General Joseph E. Johnston, Clingman managed—after first being denied because of his wound—to rejoin his troops. They were with Johnston during his retreat and ultimate surrender to Sherman at the Bennett Farmhouse, near Durham Station, on April 26.

After the war, Clingman returned to Asheville, where he resumed his law practice. He also began an earnest promotion for the development of western North Carolina and continued his prewar scientific studies of the area, including geology. In the 1850s, he had a long-running dispute with Professor Elisha Mitchell of the University of North Carolina about which peak in the Black Mountain range was the highest. During a field trip in 1857 to prove his claim, Mitchell was killed in a fall. In the 1880s, the U.S. Geological Survey upheld Mitchell's peak as the highest point in the United States east of the Rocky Mountains. The mountain now bears Mitchell's name, and he is buried there. Another peak in the Great Smoky Mountains explored and measured by Clingman is known as Clingman's Dome.

Clingman never ran for political office again, although he retained his support and loyalty to the Democratic Party and served as a delegate to the state Constitutional Convention of 1875 and to the Democratic National Convention in Saint Louis the following year. He died in Morganton, North Carolina, on November 3, 1897, and was buried at Riverside Cemetery in Asheville. He never married.

James Conner

1829–1883
Brigadier General

James Conner was born in Charleston, South Carolina, on September 1, 1829. He graduated from South Carolina College and became a lawyer. He attained the position of U.S. district attorney in 1856 and in that capacity prosecuted the case of the slave ship *Echo* in 1858. That British vessel, also claiming American registry, was apprehended by the USS *Dolphin* as it tried to land African slaves at Cuba. The slaver, out of New Orleans, had left Africa with 455 slaves on board, and 141 of them had died in the passage across the Atlantic. The United States had outlawed the international slave trade in 1808. Conner prosecuted the crew of the *Echo* for piracy according to laws of 1819 and 1820, but all of the men were acquitted.

Conner resigned as U.S. district attorney in December 1860 and lent his support to the calling of the convention that took South Carolina out of the Union in that month. The new Confederate government appointed him as a district attorney, but in the spring of 1861, he resigned that position and joined the Montgomery Guards, a South Carolina Militia unit. He was present in Charleston at the capture of Fort Sumter by Confederate forces on April 14. He soon became a captain in the Washington Light Infantry, a unit in the Hampton Legion. The legion was formed by wealthy South Carolina planter General Wade Hampton.

The legion fought in the First Battle of Manassas (or Bull Run) in July. At that Virginia battle, the Confederate army commanded by General Pierre G.T. Beauregard defeated the U.S. force led by General Irvin McDowell. Conner took over temporary command of the legion at Manassas when Hampton was wounded. He led it in the capture of Captain (later General) James B. Ricketts's artillery battery. Conner then received promotion to major and continued to serve as part of the downsized and reorganized Hampton Legion during the Peninsula Campaign (March–July 1862). In that campaign, the Confederate force, first commanded by General Joseph E. Johnston and then reorganized as the Army of Northern Virginia, led by General Robert E. Lee, opposed a Federal advance on Richmond led by General George B. McClellan. McClellan's march toward the Confederate capital progressed from the coast along the peninsula between the York and James Rivers.

In June 1862, after the Battle of Seven Pines on the peninsula, Conner was promoted to colonel and given command of the Twenty-second Regiment North Carolina Troops (originally designated the Twelfth Regiment North Carolina Volunteers). At the Battle of Mechanicsville on June 26, a rifle ball struck his leg, breaking it. He remained away from duty in the field for the next two months, convalescing for part of that time with relatives near Petersburg. Still unfit for field duty, he served as a military judge of the Second Corps of Lee's Army of Northern Virginia until he returned to his regiment at Camp Gregg, Virginia, on April 1, 1863. When his brigade commander, General Samuel McGowan, was severely wounded at the Battle of Chancellorsville (May 1–3), Conner temporarily commanded the brigade. In that battle, General Lee's Army of Northern Virginia soundly defeated the U.S. Army of the Potomac, then commanded by General Joseph Hooker.

Conner led his regiment at the famed Battle of Gettysburg, Pennsylvania (July 1–3), where the U.S. Army of the Potomac, commanded by General George G. Meade, defeated Lee's army and forced it to retreat into Virginia. In June 1864, he was promoted to brigadier general and assigned once more to lead the brigade of McGowan, who had been wounded at the Battle of Spotsylvania Court House in the previous month.

When McGowan returned to duty, Conner assumed command of General Joseph B. Kershaw's brigade, which he led in the Shenandoah Valley Campaign (August–October 1864). In that campaign, the Confederate troops of General Jubal A. Early clashed with the Federal army of General Philip H. Sheridan, which ultimately triumphed over Early's corps. On October 13, at a skirmish near Cedar Creek, Conner was wounded in the left leg. Some of his soldiers had marched too far forward, and he rode out to bring them back in line. A Federal artillery round exploded close to him, and a fragment shattered his knee, rendering him unconscious. Litter bearers carried him to an ambulance, which transported him to a field hospital. Surgeons amputated his leg close to the hip, and he never returned to duty.

After the war, Conner practiced law in South Carolina and participated in Democratic politics, which returned the state to white rule after Reconstruction. He was elected attorney general of South Carolina in 1876 and certified the election of General Wade Hampton as governor of the Palmetto State. In his final years, he served as a director and general counsel of the Greenville and Columbia Railroad. He died in Richmond, Virginia, on June 25, 1883, and was buried at Charleston's Magnolia Cemetery. In 1845, he had married Sallie Enders, and they had three children.

John Rogers Cooke

1833–1891
Brigadier General

John Rogers Cooke was born on June 9, 1833, at Jefferson Barracks, Missouri. His father, Phillip St. George Cooke, was a U.S. Army officer at the time. The elder Cooke remained loyal to the United States during the Civil War, achieved the rank of major general, and retired after fifty years in the army.

After his education as a civil engineer at Harvard University, John Rogers Cooke also joined the U.S. Army, with a commission as second lieutenant. He served in the Southwest until the secession of Virginia.

Resigning his U.S. commission, he traveled to Virginia, where, with the rank of first lieutenant, he joined the brigade of General Theophilus H. Holmes of North Carolina. Holmes's brigade participated in the First Battle of Manassas (or Bull Run) in July 1861. There the Confederate force under the command of General Pierre G.T. Beauregard defeated the Union army led by General Irvin McDowell. Following Manassas, Cooke formed a company of light artillery and deployed it in the vicinity of the Potomac River. In February 1862, he was promoted to major and assigned as chief of artillery to the Department of North Carolina, then under the command of Holmes, who had been promoted to major general in October.

On April 16, 1862, Cooke received promotion to colonel and command of the Twenty-seventh Regiment North Carolina Troops. In the previous month, the U.S. Army of the Potomac, under the leadership of General George B. McClellan, had begun threatening Richmond from the coast and along the peninsula between the York and James Rivers. A Confederate force commanded by General Joseph E. Johnston opposed McClellan's advance on the Confederate capital. This Peninsula Campaign (March–July 1862) took Holmes and his troops—including Cooke's regiment, in the brigade of General John G. Walker—to Virginia to help thwart the Union attack. At the Battle of Seven Pines (May 31–June 1), Cooke, it is believed by some, was wounded, but if so, not severely. General Johnston, however, suffered a serious wound, and General Robert E. Lee took his place, reorganizing the forces defending Richmond into the Army of Northern Virginia. Cooke's soldiers did not take part in the subsequent Seven Days Battles (June 25–July 1) and for the next two months raided Federal shipping on the Potomac.

In September, Cooke's regiment, as a unit in General Walker's demi-division of two brigades, marched with the rest of Lee's army into Maryland. It participated in the seizure of Loudon Heights at Harpers Ferry before joining Lee's main force confronting the Federal army, under McClellan, at the Battle of Sharpsburg (or Antietam) on September 17. Cooke commanded his regiment and one from Arkansas during the battle. He received orders to hold a critical point in the line at all costs, which proved to be high in the number of soldiers killed and wounded. Cooke himself was hit but did not leave the field.

Having failed to defeat McClellan, Lee's army retreated into Virginia, where Cooke soon received promotion to brigadier general. His brigade consisted of his old Twenty-seventh and four other North Carolina regiments. His soldiers began referring to themselves as Cooke's North Carolinians.

Cooke's brigade, then part of General Robert Ransom Jr.'s division, next went into action at the Battle of Fredericksburg in December 1862, where the Army of Northern Virginia dealt a devastating blow to the Army of the Potomac, then commanded by General Ambrose E. Burnside. A bullet struck Cooke above the left eye and apparently cracked his skull. Soldiers transported him from the field on a stretcher, and an ambulance carried him to the nearby home of friends, where he convalesced.

Cooke resumed command of his troops, then stationed in South Carolina, in February 1863. The brigade returned to the Tar Heel State in late April to help repel a Federal assault near Kinston. It then rushed to Virginia to join Lee's push into Pennsylvania. That operation resulted in the famed Battle of

John Rogers Cooke

Gettysburg (July 1–3), in which the Army of the Potomac, led by General George G. Meade, soundly defeated Lee's army and forced its retreat into Virginia. However, Cooke's brigade, in the division of General Henry Heth, did not fight at Gettysburg but rather remained in the vicinity to thwart Federal advances.

The brigade next went into action at the Battle of Bristoe Station, Virginia, in October 1863. Cooke opposed the action, which proved disastrous for Lee's Third Corps, led by General A.P. Hill. Cooke's troops sustained heavy casualties, and his shinbone was shattered. He recovered from the wound and returned to duty in the middle of April 1864.

Under the impetus of the new general in chief of the U.S. Army, Ulysses S. Grant, the Army of the Potomac, with Meade in tactical command and accompanied by Grant, began an unrelenting campaign to push Lee's army back to Richmond and force its ultimate surrender. On the first day of the Battle of the Wilderness (May 5–6, 1864), Cooke's brigade was heavily engaged and lost a large number of men. Cooke was badly wounded and continued to suffer from his injuries as his troops went into the trenches at the Siege of Petersburg, just south of Richmond. In that area, Cooke and his soldiers participated in a number of operations, including the Battle of Reams's Station. Lee himself praised the brigade for its performance in that action.

On April 2, 1865, the Army of the Potomac broke through Lee's defenses at Petersburg and forced the Confederate army to flee westward. In the retreat, Cooke found himself in charge of four small brigades. The Federals captured much of his command at Sutherland's Station. But part, including Cooke himself, escaped and was present when Lee surrendered to Grant at Appomattox Court House on April 9.

Students of the Civil War generally regard Cooke as a capable commander. Robert E. Lee considered him one of his best brigadiers. Although not a native North Carolinian, Cooke was respected and admired by the Tar Heel troops who served under him. His family exemplified the types of divisions that the war caused many families. His father fought for the Union as a general. His sister Flora married the famed Confederate general J.E.B. Stuart, and another sister, Maria, married Confederate surgeon Charles Brewer. A third sister, Julia, became the wife of Brevet Brigadier General Jacob Sharpe of the U.S. Army.

After the war, Cooke launched a mercantile business in Richmond and became active in the city's Democratic politics. He served as director of the chamber of commerce and as president of Virginia's state prison. He was founder and manager of Richmond's Confederate Soldiers' Home and a commander of the local camp of the United Confederate Veterans. Cooke was married to Nannie G. Patton of Fredericksburg, Virginia, and they had eight children. He died in Richmond on April 10, 1891, and was buried at that city's Hollywood Cemetery.

William Ruffin Cox

1832–1919
Brigadier General

William Ruffin Cox was born in Scotland Neck, North Carolina, on March 11, 1832. His early education took place at the Vine Hill Academy in that town. After the death of his father, his mother moved the family to Nashville, Tennessee. There he continued his education and entered Franklin College, from which he graduated in 1850. He then studied law at Lebanon College, also in Tennessee. Admitted to the bar, he practiced law in Nashville for five years. Shortly after marrying Penelope Battle, daughter of Edgecombe County planter James S. Battle, in 1857, Cox

moved back to North Carolina, where he established a large plantation, Penelo, in that county. He moved to Raleigh two years later and launched a successful law practice, dividing his time and attention between that and his plantation.

Cox adhered to strong southern rights and secession views. When the Civil War broke out, he immediately formed and financed an artillery company. But he soon became an infantry officer when he received a commission as major in the Second Regiment North Carolina State Troops.

During the Seven Days Battles (June 25–July 1), when the Army of Northern Virginia, led by General Robert E. Lee, counterattacked the advance toward Richmond by the U.S. Army of the Potomac, commanded by General George B. McClellan, Cox fought at the Battles of Mechanicsville and Malvern Hill. He was wounded at the latter and remained out of action until September, returning to duty in time to participate in the Battle of Sharpsburg (or Antietam) on September 17, after which he received promotion to lieutenant colonel. At Sharpsburg, McClellan's army halted Lee's advance into Maryland and forced his retreat into Virginia. Cox's quick promotion to full colonel followed the Battle of Fredericksburg in December 1862. That proved to be a victory for Lee's Confederates, who inflicted heavy losses on the Army of the Potomac, then commanded by General Ambrose E. Burnside.

At the Battle of Chancellorsville in May 1863, the Army of Northern Virginia again triumphed over the Army of the Potomac, then led by still another commander, General Joseph Hooker. During the fighting, Cox received five or six wounds but stayed with his regiment as long as possible. He recovered sufficiently to participate in action in November along the Rappahannock River. There he was wounded in the right shoulder and face. He had hospital treatment at Richmond before going on a medical leave of absence.

Cox next returned to combat at the Battle of Spotsylvania Court House in May 1864. That struggle pitted Lee's Confederates against the Army of the Potomac, then with General George G. Meade in tactical command and General in Chief Ulysses S. Grant in overall command. In Grant's Overland Campaign (May–June), the Federals were attempting to drive Lee back toward Richmond and ultimate surrender, but they were repulsed after severe fighting at Spotsylvania. In that battle, Cox's Second Regiment protected the right center of the brigade of General Stephen Dodson Ramseur. Despite an enfilading fire that inflicted heavy casualties, the Second forced two lines of Union infantry to flee the field.

The Army of Northern Virginia and the Army of the Potomac again locked in fierce combat at the Battle of Cold Harbor in June. The Union troops suffered massive numbers killed and wounded as the result of a frontal assault on Lee's lines. Shortly after the battle, Cox received promotion to brigadier general and command of Ramseur's brigade, after its commander was promoted to major general and assigned to lead a division.

As part of Ramseur's division, Cox's brigade, composed of six North Carolina regiments, fought in the Shenandoah Valley Campaign (August

1864–March 1865). That months-long conflict involved fighting between the Confederate corps led by General Jubal A. Early and the Army of the Shenandoah, commanded by General Philip H. Sheridan. The Union army ultimately vanquished Early's force, closing a major area of supply and avenue of attack for the Confederacy. Sheridan's victory marked the beginning of the end for Lee's army in Virginia, the major portion of which had in the meantime entered defensive works near Petersburg.

Cox's brigade joined the rest of the Army of Northern Virginia around Petersburg and was part of its flight westward when Lee was finally forced to abandon his trenches. Cox and his men were with Lee when he surrendered to Grant at Appomattox Court House on April 9, 1865. Near that site, Cox's troops are credited with making the last organized attack by the Army of Northern Virginia before the surrender.

After the war, Cox returned to his Raleigh law practice and began reviving Penelo. He became president of the board of the Chatham Coal Fields Railway. He opposed Republicans' Congressional Reconstruction policies and became active in the Conservative (or Democratic) Party's efforts to regain control in postwar North Carolina. In 1868, he was elected state solicitor for the Raleigh District and served six years. He became chairman of the Democratic Party in 1874 and worked hard for "redemption" of the Tar Heel State from Republican rule. He declined to run for governor in 1876, conceding the Democratic nomination to Zebulon B. Vance, who then appointed him judge of the Sixth Judicial District of North Carolina, a position he held until 1880. Cox was also chairman of the North Carolina Education Association in the 1870s.

From 1884 to 1887, he served in the U.S. House of Representatives, where, as chairman of the Committee on Civil Service, he called for reform in the federal civil service. In 1893, he was elected secretary of the U.S. Senate, and he remained at that post until 1906, when he returned to North Carolina.

After the death of his first wife, Cox married Frances August Lyman in 1883. When she, too, preceded him in death, he married the widow Mrs. Herbert A. Claiborne of Richmond in 1905. His first marriage produced one son, who died in early manhood, and his second marriage resulted in two other sons. Cox died in Richmond on December 26, 1919, and was buried at Oakwood Cemetery in Raleigh. Although lacking any prewar military training, Cox gave a credible performance as a brigadier general for the Confederacy, being twice praised by General Lee.

Junius Daniel

1828–1864
Brigadier General

Junius Daniel was born in Halifax County, North Carolina, on June 27, 1828. He received an elementary education there and then attended the academy of Jefferson M. Lovejoy in Raleigh. He gained an appointment to the U.S. Military Academy at West Point in 1846 and graduated in 1851. His graduation was delayed a year because of injuries he sustained in an artillery practice. Daniel saw service in the U.S. Army at Newport, Kentucky, and Fort Albuquerque, New Mexico, before resigning his commission in 1858 to manage his father's plantation in Louisiana.

Upon North Carolina's secession, he returned to his native state and became colonel of the Fourteenth Regiment North Carolina Troops (originally designated the Fourth Regiment North Carolina Volunteers). In September 1861, illness forced him to take a leave of absence, but he resumed his duties in November as his regiment performed operations in North Carolina. In April 1862, he was appointed colonel of the Forty-fifth Regiment North Carolina Troops. The following month, he was given command of a newly formed brigade that included three Tar Heel regiments. The brigade moved to Virginia and joined the Seven Days Battles (June 25–July 1), in which General Robert E. Lee's Army of Northern Virginia counterattacked and halted the Army of the Potomac, led by General George B. McClellan, as it advanced toward Richmond from the coast. During the final battle of the Seven Days at Malvern Hill, a Federal shell exploded near Daniel, knocking him from his horse. Stunned, he struggled to a gatepost close by to recover his senses. He then secured another horse and rejoined the battle. Daniel officially received his commission as brigadier general on September 1, 1862.

Daniel and his brigade, which had been expanded by two regiments, returned to duty in North Carolina the following winter. In March 1863, Daniel led his troops in an assault by General D.H. Hill to recapture the town of New Bern, which had been held by the Federal army since March of the previous year. Hill came under the departmental command of General James Longstreet, who ordered the attack on New Bern. That operation was poorly executed and largely failed. According to historian Douglas Southall Freeman, it "scarcely deserved to be called anything more than a reconnaissance in force."

Nevertheless, Daniel's brigade performed well, achieving perhaps the only success of the whole Confederate effort. His soldiers were the first to strike the Union defenses at the coastal town. They overran the Federal works at Deep Gully, a site where U.S. troops protected the rail line leading into New Bern along the area between the Neuse and Trent Rivers. At dawn the following day, they beat off a Federal effort to recapture the entrenchments and held their position until the overall failure of the Confederate expedition forced them to withdraw with the rest of Hill's force. Daniel's brigade also participated in Hill's subsequent attempt to retake the town of Washington, North Carolina, by siege, but that operation, too, proved unsuccessful for the Confederates.

In May 1863, Daniel's brigade returned to the Army of Northern Virginia as part of General Robert E. Rodes's division and fought at the Battle of Gettysburg in July. There the Army of the Potomac, then commanded by General George G. Meade, halted Lee's advance into Pennsylvania and dealt him a major defeat, forcing the Army of Northern Virginia to retreat into Virginia. Later that month, an ill Daniel gave up command of his brigade and entered a general hospital in Charlottesville, where he was diagnosed with "hepatitic derangement." He returned to duty in September.

Daniel led his brigade in the Battle of the Wilderness (May 5–6, 1864), in which the Army of the Potomac, with Meade in tactical command and accompanied by General in Chief Ulysses S. Grant, attempted to press Lee's army back toward Richmond. Grant, in this Overland Campaign (May–

June), hoped to effect Lee's surrender. Although the Federals ultimately forced Lee's army into entrenchments at Petersburg, the Confederates made them pay a heavy price in casualties, especially at the Battle of Cold Harbor (June 1–3). Earlier, at the Battle of Spotsylvania Court House, Lee's troops had repulsed the Army of the Potomac. It was during the fighting there on May 12 that Daniel was mortally wounded in the abdomen, and he died the next day.

Daniel's body was taken back to Halifax, North Carolina, where he was buried at the Old Colonial Churchyard cemetery. Daniel had married Ellen Long of Northampton County in 1860. They had no children.

Daniel Gould Fowle

1831–1891
State Adjutant General and Major General of Militia

D aniel Gould Fowle was born on March 3, 1831, in Washington, North Carolina. He attended the academy of William J. Bingham in Hillsborough before enrolling at Princeton University at the age of fourteen. There he became a member of the Literary Society and a junior orator, graduating in 1851. Fowle studied law with the famed North Carolina jurist Richmond M. Pearson. Admitted to the bar, he established a law practice in Raleigh.

Fowle originally opposed secession, but once the war began, he joined the Raleigh Rifles as a private and soon rose to second lieutenant. He left that unit to join the state Commissary Department, with the rank of major. He soon resigned to become lieutenant colonel of the Thirty-first Regiment North Carolina Troops. The regiment took part in the Battle of Roanoke Island in February 1862, in which a Confederate force defended the island against a Federal expedition led by General Ambrose E. Burnside. The Union army easily overwhelmed the defenders, took the island, and went on to secure and occupy much of coastal North Carolina. Fowle was captured and remained a prisoner of war for two weeks before being paroled.

He failed to win election as colonel of the Thirty-first and resigned from the Confederate army in September 1862, just in time to serve a term in the General Assembly. When the session ended, Governor Zebulon B. Vance appointed him adjutant general of North Carolina, with the rank of major general of Militia. Fowle resigned that position in August 1863 after Vance revoked his general order that all communications to the governor that pertained to the state's war effort should pass through the adjutant general's office. To Vance's assertion that the order was unlawful, Fowle responded: "I beg leave to say in this...opinion you are mistaken." The governor immediately accepted the general's resignation and appointed Richard Caswell Gatlin the new adjutant general. Fowle was reelected to the state legislature and served until the war's end.

At the outset of Presidential Reconstruction in 1865, Fowle was appointed a state superior court judge, but he resigned that position when Congress established new Reconstruction policies and military rule in the South in 1867. He then practiced law and became active in Democratic (formerly Conservative) Party politics, serving as state chairman. He ran for governor as a Democrat in 1880 but lost the party nomination to Thomas Jordan Jarvis. He also lost his bid as the party's candidate for a seat in Congress in 1884.

Political success finally came when Fowle was elected governor of the Tar Heel State in 1889. His efforts to bring about railroad reform had little success, and he did not live to preside over the newly established Railroad Commission. But Fowle had better results in education. He recommended a tax to support public education in counties unable to maintain public schools for the required four months per year. He also called for the creation of a state university for women, and in February 1891, the legislature chartered the State Normal and Industrial School for Women (the present-day University of North Carolina at Greensboro). Fowle was the first governor to live in the Executive Mansion in Raleigh, which is still the residence of North Carolina's governors. He moved into the dwelling in January 1891, although construction was not complete. He died on April 8, 1891, only three months later, and was buried at Raleigh's Oakwood Cemetery. Lieutenant Governor Thomas Michael Holt served out Fowle's gubernatorial term.

Fowle had married Ellen Brent Pearson, the daughter of his law mentor, Richmond Pearson, in 1856. They had two daughters before she died, six years later. He then married Mary E. Haywood of Raleigh in 1867, and they had four children. She did not live to move into the new governor's residence with him, and their daughter Helen served as hostess.

Richard Caswell Gatlin

1809–1896
State Adjutant General, Major General of Militia, and Brigadier General

Richard Caswell Gatlin was born at Kinston, in Lenoir County, North Carolina. He attended the University of North Carolina in 1824–25 before being accepted at the U.S. Military Academy at West Point, from which he graduated in 1834. Commissioned a second lieutenant, he joined the Seventh U.S. Infantry Regiment and was posted on the western frontier. He received promotion to first lieutenant in 1836. He saw further service in the Second Seminole War (1835–42) and then in Louisiana and Texas, being promoted to captain in the latter state. During the Mexican-American War (1846–48), he was wounded at the Battle of Monterrey and received the brevet rank of major for his performance.

After the war with Mexico, Gatlin served in Missouri, Louisiana, Florida, Kansas, and the Indian Territory (present Oklahoma); with the U.S. Army's expedition against the Mormons in Utah in 1857; and at Fort Craig, New Mexico, where he received the permanent rank of major in the Fifth U.S. Infantry. While visiting Arkansas in April 1861, he was taken prisoner by Arkansas state troops as that state gravitated toward secession. Soon paroled, he resigned his U.S. commission and returned to North Carolina, where he accepted appointment as state adjutant general, with the rank of major general of Militia.

Gatlin served in that capacity for only a short time, resigning to accept a commission as a colonel in the Confederate army. In August 1861, he was promoted to brigadier general and given command of the Department of North Carolina, with the assignment of preparing the coastal defenses of the state, an overwhelming task given the vast area of sounds, rivers, and barrier islands and the limited resources of men, weapons, equipment, gunboats, and supplies.

The U.S. Army easily defeated the Confederate troops defending Hatteras Island in August 1861 and then, commanded by General Ambrose E. Burnside, captured Roanoke Island in February and New Bern on March 14, 1862. Having gained those footholds, the Federals occupied much of the Tar Heel coast until the end of the war. Gatlin received a large part of the blame for the poor coastal defense and the battle defeats. He was even accused—erroneously—of being drunk during the Battle of New Bern. He countered that "these failures do not by right rest with me." He blamed his lack of success on the Confederate War Department in Richmond for refusing his requests for reinforcements and supplies. He had pleaded, he said, "until he was ashamed to ask further."

Gatlin had been suffering from ill health for some months and was confined to bed at his headquarters in Goldsboro during March. On the nineteenth of that month, he was relieved of command at his own request, citing sickness as his reason. In September, he resigned his Confederate commission as brigadier. He then returned to his earlier position as state adjutant general and served in that capacity until the end of the war.

At that time, he moved to Arkansas and began farming in Sebastian County. He relocated to Fort Smith in 1881 and died at Mount Nebo in Nebo, Arkansas, on September 8, 1896. He married his first wife, Scioto, in 1852, and she died in childbirth. He then married Mary Ann Gibson. Both his wives and two children are buried at the same cemetery as he, in Fort Smith.

Jeremy Francis Gilmer

1818–1883
Major General

Jeremy Francis Gilmer was born in Guilford County on February 23, 1818. He graduated from the U.S. Military Academy at West Point in 1839, fourth in a class of thirty-one cadets. He was commissioned a second lieutenant of engineers and would spend his entire military career as an engineer. He served first as an assistant professor of engineering at West Point and then undertook various engineering assignments for the U.S. Army in New York and Washington, D.C., and during the Mexican-American War (1846–48), as well as throughout the South. In 1858, the army transferred him to the West Coast, where he supervised the construction of defenses in San Francisco Bay.

After newly formed Confederate forces fired on Fort Sumter, South Carolina, in April 1861 and President Lincoln called on the states for troops to suppress the rebellion, Gilmer resigned his U.S. commission and traveled to Savannah, Georgia, arriving there in October. He received a commission in the Confederate army as a major of engineers and joined the staff of General Albert Sidney Johnston's Army of Tennessee. In the western theater of war, he supervised construction of fortifications at Nashville, Clarksville, Fort Donelson on the Cumberland River, and Fort Henry on the Tennessee River.

Gilmer was wounded at the Battle of Pittsburg Landing (or Shiloh) in Tennessee on April 7, 1862. At that battle, the U.S. force, commanded by General Ulysses S. Grant, won a hard-fought victory over the force of Johnston, who was killed in action and replaced by General Pierre G.T. Beauregard. A bullet fractured Gilmer's right arm, and he was transferred to Savannah to recover. Although his wound had almost healed by June, severe rheumatism and the need for dental work kept him in Georgia until August. Having just been promoted to lieutenant colonel, he then joined the Army of Northern Virginia and took charge of the defenses in the Richmond-Petersburg area. In October, he was promoted to colonel and made chief of the Confederate War Department's Engineer Bureau, a position he held for the rest of the war. His rheumatism continued to plague him, and at times he could not raise his wounded arm.

In August 1863, Gilmer received promotion to major general, and the secretary of war soon dispatched him south to inspect the Confederacy's Atlantic defenses. He made inspections and supervised improvements at Charleston, Savannah, Atlanta, and Mobile. He also served as second in command of the Department of South Carolina, Georgia, and Florida. During his tour, Gilmer developed trouble with his eyes and was hospitalized in Savannah for a time. In June 1864, he returned to Richmond, where he managed the Engineer Bureau until the end of the war. At that time, he fled the Confederate capital with President Davis and his cabinet.

Gilmer proved to be a capable military engineer for the Confederacy. He demonstrated effective administrative ability in a bureau with limited resources, and he cooperated well with the president and the secretary of war. He organized engineer units, provided specific guidelines, and called for engineer activity to be regulated by the bureau. In the *Army Regulations*, he published General Order 90, which specified the duties and responsibilities of the army's engineers.

After the war, Gilmer lived in Georgia and became president of the Savannah Gas Light Company and a director of the Central Railroad and Banking Company. He had married Georgian Louisa Frederika Alexander in 1850, and they had two children. He died on December 1, 1883, and was buried at Savannah's Laurel Grove Cemetery.

Archibald Campbell Godwin

1831–1864
Brigadier General

Archibald Campbell Godwin was born in Nansemond County, Virginia, on September 19, 1831. His family moved to Portsmouth when he was only one year old. After his father died, his grandmother, Julia Hatton Godwin, raised him. In 1849, he left home to seek his fortune in the California gold rush. He worked for a time as a miner and engaged in ranching and the lumber and milling businesses, eventually acquiring a sizable fortune. He owned a large part of Vancouver Island but relinquished it to Canada when the western boundary between that country and the United States was settled. Godwin ran for governor of California in 1860 but failed by a narrow margin to win the Democratic nomination.

With the outbreak of the Civil War, he turned over his business interests to associates and returned to Virginia, where he received a commission as major in the Confederate army and an assignment as assistant provost marshal at Libby Prison in Richmond. His success there led the War Department to send him to North Carolina to establish a prisoner-of-war stockade at Salisbury. He served as commandant of that prison for captured Union soldiers. In July 1862, he organized the Fifty-seventh Regiment North

Carolina Troops from among the soldiers guarding the prison and received the rank of colonel of that unit.

Godwin's new regiment transferred to the Richmond area, where, in the brigade of General Joseph R. Davis and the division of General Gustavus M. Smith, it drilled and defended the Confederate capital. During the early autumn, Godwin took a short medical furlough, suffering from jaundice. He and his men joined General Robert E. Lee's Army of Northern Virginia in November and the following month took part in the Battle of Fredericksburg as part of the brigade of General Evander M. Law and the division of General John B. Hood. At Fredericksburg, Lee's army inflicted a devastating defeat on the Army of the Potomac, then led by General Ambrose E. Burnside. For their performance in the battle, Godwin and his soldiers received the praise of both Hood and Lee.

In April 1863, Godwin's regiment transferred to the brigade of General Robert F. Hoke in the division of General Jubal A. Early, and it fought in the Battle of Chancellorsville the following month. There General Lee's army dealt a severe blow to the Army of the Potomac, then commanded by General Joseph Hooker. During that action, Godwin's troops fought in the vicinity of Fredericksburg. On May 4, Godwin was wounded slightly in the knee, but he had returned to duty by June.

When Lee's force faced the Army of the Potomac, then led by General George G. Meade, at the Battle of Gettysburg, Pennsylvania, in July, Hoke's brigade was under the command of Colonel Isaac Avery while Hoke recovered from wounds. When Avery himself was wounded, command of the brigade fell to Godwin as the senior colonel. Gettysburg proved to be a disaster for Lee, whose troops fled back to Virginia.

Still commanding the brigade of Hoke, who had recovered but was on special assignment in North Carolina, Godwin led his troops in the fighting around Bristoe Station and the Rappahannock River in autumn. A Federal attack on the Rappahannock Bridge on November 7 overwhelmed Godwin's brigade, and U.S. troops took him and many of his soldiers prisoner. The Federals held him at the Johnson's Island Prison in Ohio. That his superiors made considerable effort to have him exchanged testifies to his worth as a combat leader, despite a lack of prewar military experience. He was exchanged in the spring of 1864 and, after recovering from illness in a Charlottesville hospital, rejoined Early's division for fighting in the Shenandoah Valley. He received promotion to brigadier general in August. On September 19, he was leading troops at the Third Battle of Winchester when a fragment from a Union artillery shell struck him in the head, killing him instantly. He was buried in Winchester.

James Byron Gordon

1822–1864
Brigadier General

James Byron Gordon was born at Wilkesboro, North Carolina, on November 2, 1822. He attended the school run by Peter Stuart Ney in Iredell County, and then Emory and Henry College in Virginia for two or three years, before returning to Wilkesboro to join his family's mercantile business and supervise the farming operations. He represented Wilkes County in the state legislature in 1850.

As North Carolina secession loomed after Confederates fired on Fort Sumter, South Carolina, in April 1861 and President Lincoln called for troops to suppress the rebellion, Gordon enlisted as a private in the Wilkes County Guards. He became a first lieutenant when that unit was organized as Company B of the First Regiment North Carolina Cavalry. The cavalry regiment was then organized again as the Ninth Regiment North Carolina State Troops at Camp Beauregard in Warren County in August 1861. Gordon received an appointment as major in the new regiment, commanded by Colonel Robert Ransom Jr., with Lieutenant Colonel Laurence S. Baker as second in command.

The Ninth Regiment North Carolina State Troops (First Regiment North Carolina Cavalry) transferred in October to Richmond and then Manassas Junction in Virginia as part of General J.E.B. Stuart's cavalry. The regiment performed primarily scouting and guard duty until it was ordered back to North Carolina in March 1862 to help oppose an anticipated Federal attack in the eastern part of the state. A U.S. expedition led by General Ambrose E. Burnside had recently captured Roanoke Island and New Bern and occupied a large part of the coastal region, posing a threat to the interior of the state. Gordon's regiment soon returned to Virginia to participate in the Peninsula Campaign (March–July), in which a U.S. invasion led by General George B. McClellan advanced toward Richmond along the peninsula between the York and James Rivers.

Originally, General Joseph E. Johnston commanded the Confederate force opposing McClellan, but he had to be relieved when he was wounded at the Battle of Seven Pines on May 31. His replacement, General Robert E. Lee, reorganized the Confederate units into the Army of Northern Virginia, dividing the cavalry into two brigades under the overall leadership of Stuart. Gordon's regiment was assigned to the brigade commanded by General Wade Hampton of South Carolina. In the meantime, Ransom had transferred to the infantry, and Baker became colonel of the Ninth Regiment (First Cavalry). Gordon then became lieutenant colonel and second in command. The regiment participated in the Army of Northern Virginia's successful efforts to drive McClellan from the peninsula in a series of actions known as the Seven Days Battles (June 25–July 1).

Gordon's regiment remained behind to guard Richmond when Lee's army defeated the U.S. Army of Virginia, commanded by General John Pope, at the Second Battle of Manassas, Virginia, in August. The regiment rejoined the Army of Northern Virginia on September 2, in time for the invasion of Maryland. It did not participate in the subsequent Battle of Sharpsburg (or Antietam), where General McClellan and the Army of the Potomac halted Lee's army and forced its retreat into Virginia. But the Ninth did engage in skirmishes as the Confederate cavalry reconnoitered the Federals and screened Lee's retreating column.

During the Confederate triumph at the Battle of Fredericksburg in December, Gordon's brigade attacked the supply lines of Burnside, who had replaced McClellan in command of the Army of the Potomac. Because of Burnside's defeat by Lee at Fredericksburg, the U.S. War Department replaced him with General Joseph E. Hooker. Lee decisively defeated Hooker at the Battle of Chancellorsville in May 1863, but during that battle, Gordon's regiment was "south of the James River recruiting." It then assembled with the rest of the Army of Northern Virginia and fought at the Battle of Brandy Station in early June. During the fighting, the Ninth Regiment (First Cavalry) routed the Tenth Regiment New York Cavalry and captured its standard.

When Lee's army invaded Pennsylvania and clashed with the Army of the Potomac, then commanded by General George G. Meade, at the famed Battle of Gettysburg in July, Gordon's regiment was part of General Stuart's "ride around" the Union army. At an engagement in the Federal rear on July 3, Hampton was wounded, and Baker became commander of the brigade. Gordon then took command of his regiment and continued to lead it as Lee's defeated army retreated into Virginia. General Stuart praised his leadership, reporting that he exhibited "individual prowess deserving special commendation." Gordon officially received promotion to full colonel on August 11 and was temporarily assigned to command the Nineteenth Regiment North Carolina Troops (Second Regiment North Carolina Cavalry). But he soon returned to the Ninth and even commanded Hampton's entire brigade in action near Jack's Shop on September 22.

A few days later, he was promoted to brigadier general and given command of a new brigade made up of five North Carolina cavalry regiments, including his old Ninth (First Cavalry). Baker had been the unit's original brigadier, but he had been wounded and left field service. Stuart and Lee quickly filled the vacancy with Gordon.

In early October, Lee crossed the Rappahannock River and engaged Meade in an action known as the Bristoe Campaign, which lasted until the twentieth of the month. During that operation, Gordon's troops fought in a number of engagements in Virginia. Near Warrenton Road on October 14, a bullet cut a small blood vessel in the general's nose. He bled profusely but was not long absent from duty. Five days later, he led his brigade in a battle at Buckland Mills, near Warrenton, known as the Buckland Races. The Confederate attack routed the Union cavalry. At the subsequent Mine Run Campaign (November 27–December 2)—when Lee drove Meade back across the Rapidan River—Gordon had his horse shot from under him near a place called Parker's Store. Both armies then went into winter camp, although in March 1864, Gordon's men helped turn back a Union cavalry raid on Richmond led by General Judson Kilpatrick and Colonel Ulric Dahlgren.

When the Army of the Potomac was next on the move in the spring, it was accompanied by Ulysses S. Grant, general in chief of the Union army.

Meade remained in direct tactical command as Grant began his Overland Campaign (May–June 1864) to press Lee's Army of Northern Virginia back toward Richmond and ultimate surrender. Federal officers began moving the army across the Rapidan River on May 4. About that time, Gordon's brigade was transferred from Hampton's division to that of General William H.F. Lee. Stuart had commanded Robert E. Lee's entire cavalry corps, which included those divisions, since Gettysburg.

During the ensuing Battles of the Wilderness (May 5–6) and Spotsylvania Court House (May 7–19), Gordon's brigade assisted in checking Grant's advance, reporting Federal movement, protecting the infantry, and taking prisoners. When General Philip H. Sheridan and twelve thousand Yankee horsemen launched a raid toward Richmond on May 9, Gordon's troops undertook the assignment of "harassing the enemy and impeding his progress. This involved incessant fighting, both day and night, with losses of men and animals." With other cavalry brigades, Stuart managed to get in front of the Federals and stop their advance. But the dashing Confederate cavalry corps commander was mortally wounded at Yellow Tavern on May 11. At the height of battle, just before being struck by a pistol bullet, he reportedly declared, "Would to God, Gordon were here."

That North Carolinian himself would not survive much longer. With his troops locked in combat with Sheridan's force at Meadow Bridge on May 12, Gordon was urging his horse soldiers to stand fast until infantry reinforcements could arrive when a minié ball struck him in the arm. Transferred to a hospital in Richmond, he lived only a few days. His body was transported back to Wilkesboro and buried at St. Paul's Episcopal Church cemetery. He had no heirs.

Bryan Grimes

1828–1880
Major General

Bryan Grimes was born on November 2, 1828, on a large Pitt County plantation known as Grimesland. He attended schools in Nash County and Washington, North Carolina, before becoming a student at the noted Hillsborough school of William James Bingham. At age fifteen, he enrolled at the University of North Carolina at Chapel Hill, from which he graduated in 1848. In the following year, his father awarded him Grimesland plantation and one hundred slaves, and he began managing the agricultural enterprise. He traveled abroad in 1860 and returned to North Carolina as the sectional crisis was coming to a head and the nation was on the brink of civil war.

After Confederate troops in South Carolina fired on Fort Sumter in April 1861 and President Lincoln asked the states still in the Union for troops to suppress the rebellion, North Carolina voters called for a Secession Convention to consider withdrawing from the United States. Grimes was elected a delegate to that convention, where he strongly supported secession. He believed in the superiority of Southerners and Southern culture and held contempt for Northerners and their customs. He was once reported to have "unflinching hostility to all Yankees—Yankee notions—& Yankee sympathizers." On May 20, 1861, the delegates passed the Ordinance of Secession, and North Carolina soon joined the other seceded states in the new Confederate States of America.

Grimes accepted a commission as major in the Fourth Regiment North Carolina State Troops, an infantry unit. He accompanied his regiment to Virginia, arriving in the vicinity of Manassas Junction following the First Battle of Manassas (or Bull Run) in July 1861. He received promotion to lieutenant colonel in May 1862, in time to participate in the Battle of Seven Pines (May 31–June 1). That struggle occurred during the Peninsula Campaign (May–June), in which the Confederate forces, originally commanded by General Joseph E. Johnston, attempted to halt the advance on Richmond by General George B. McClellan and the Army of the Potomac. During the battle, Federal fire killed Grimes's horse, which fell on his leg, but he was not injured. Grimes, in fact, was the only officer in his regiment to escape being wounded. Of the regiment's 520 men, 462 became casualties. Johnston himself was wounded, relinquishing command of the Confederate troops in Virginia to General Robert E. Lee, who reorganized them as the Army of Northern Virginia. Grimes received official promotion to full colonel and command of his regiment on June 19.

Grimes and the Fourth Infantry fought in the Seven Days Battles (June 25–July 1) that ensued as Lee attempted to thwart McClellan's assault toward the Confederate capital and force his withdrawal from the peninsula between the York and James Rivers. Grimes and his troops particularly distinguished themselves at the Battle of Mechanicsville on June 26. During the Seven Days fighting, his brigade commander proclaimed that "Colonel Grimes and his regiment are the keystone of my brigade."

About mid-July, Grimes contracted typhoid fever and withdrew to Raleigh, North Carolina, to recuperate. He returned to Virginia in time to join the Army of Northern Virginia's invasion of Maryland. But as his unit crossed the Potomac River near Edward's Ferry on September 5, a horse kicked him severely on the leg. Because he could not ride or walk, he was transported for a time in an ambulance.

On September 14, as the Army of Northern Virginia approached a showdown with McClellan's Army of the Potomac at the Battle of Sharpsburg (or Antietam), Grimes managed to mount his horse and fight in an action at South Mountain. Again his horse was killed, and for a while, he commanded on foot. Because of his persistent leg injury, however, he had to be taken to a hospital in Shepherdstown and then Winchester, Virginia. He thus missed the Battle of Sharpsburg on the seventeenth. In that battle, McClellan forced

Lee's retreat into Virginia. Surgeons came close to amputating Grimes's leg but ultimately decided not to operate. He remained at Winchester until he returned to field duty in November.

At the Battle of Fredericksburg in December 1862, Grimes temporarily commanded a brigade in the division of General D.H. Hill, as Lee's army dealt a devastating blow to the Army of the Potomac, then commanded by General Ambrose E. Burnside. During the Battle of Chancellorsville in early May 1863, Lee again defeated the Army of the Potomac, this time led by General Joseph Hooker. Grimes led his regiment with skill. A bullet broke his sword, several rounds perforated his clothes, and he severely bruised his foot. He passed out from exhaustion and pain. Soldiers revived him by pouring water over his head and transported him by litter to a field hospital. Although he rode a horse the following day, his foot injury continued to plague him.

When the Army of Northern Virginia invaded Pennsylvania on its way to the famed Battle of Gettysburg in July, Grimes had to ride in an ambulance most of the way because of his lamed foot. At Gettysburg, the Army of the Potomac, then commanded by General George G. Meade, defeated Lee's force and drove it back into Virginia. Grimes led the Fourth Regiment in the fight, but during the retreat, he fell ill near Martinsburg and rode with the wagons.

The rest of 1863 passed relatively quietly for Grimes, although he presided over a meeting of North Carolina soldiers in response to the growing peace movement taking place in North Carolina. A confirmed Southern rights advocate and Confederate, Grimes condemned the peace campaign and its leader, Raleigh newspaper editor William W. Holden. He continued to express his loathing of Northerners, especially soldiers. He referred to Federal prisoners as "the lowest scum of the Yankee population."

Grimes and his regiment fought well at the Battle of Spotsylvania Court House (May 7–19, 1864). That battle was a result of General Ulysses S. Grant's Overland Campaign (May–June) for the Army of the Potomac to press the Army of Northern Virginia back toward Richmond and force its surrender. During the campaign, Grant, who was then general in chief of the U.S. Army, accompanied the Army of the Potomac, of which General Meade remained in tactical command. During the fighting at Spotsylvania, Grimes took over leadership of the brigade of General Stephen Dodson Ramseur, who had been wounded, and led a charge at the Bloody Angle. On May 19, Grimes received promotion to brigadier general and command of the old brigade of General Junius Daniel, who had been killed at Spotsylvania.

Grimes suffered from rheumatism and bowel problems in the next two months and was hospitalized in Lynchburg in July. He returned to duty on August 6—although a surgeon had certified that he was not fit for service—in time to lead his brigade in the Shenandoah Valley Campaign (August 7, 1864–March 2, 1865), which pitted the Confederate army of General Jubal A. Early against the Union army of General Philip H. Sheridan. While in action at Strasburg on September 22, Grimes, anticipating fighting on foot, dismounted and sprained his ankle as he attempted to enter a trench. Finding his soldiers nearly surrounded, he ordered a retreat, but because of his ankle injury, he almost did not escape capture. At the Battle of Cedar Creek on October 19, Grimes took command of the division of General Ramseur, who had fallen mortally wounded. Permanent promotion to major general followed for Grimes on February 23, 1865.

He then led troops at the Siege of Petersburg, as Lee undertook his last-ditch defense of Richmond against Grant's onslaught. Grimes was present at the surrender of the Army of Northern Virginia at Appomattox Court House in April, having led one of the last Confederate assaults on the Army of the Potomac.

After the war, Grimes returned to his Pitt County plantation. He became a trustee of the University of North Carolina in 1877. In 1851, he had married Elizabeth Hilliard Davis, who died six years later. He then married Charlotte Emily Bryan in 1863. Both marriages produced a number of children. In August 1880, Grimes was returning to Grimesland from Washington, North Carolina, when an assassin named William Parker shot and killed him. The motive apparently was to keep Grimes from testifying in a court case. A jury acquitted Parker of the murder, but a Washington lynch mob hanged him from a drawbridge over the Pamlico River in 1888. Grimes was buried at Grimesland.

Daniel Harvey Hill

1821–1889

Major General and Lieutenant General (Temporary and Unconfirmed)

Daniel Harvey Hill was born in York District, South Carolina, on July 12, 1821. After his father's early death, he and his ten older siblings were raised by their mother, who imparted to him a strong religious conviction. Hill entered the U.S. Military Academy at West Point in 1838, graduating four years later twenty-eighth in a class of fifty-six. He then served in two U.S. Army artillery regiments.

During the Mexican-American War (1846–48), he served first under General Zachary Taylor at Monterrey and then under General Winfield Scott at Mexico City. He received permanent promotion to first lieutenant in March 1857 and brevets as captain and major for his performance at Contreras and Chapultepec, respectively. The State of South Carolina awarded him a gold sword for his service in the war.

Hill left the army in February 1849 and became a professor of mathematics at Washington College (present-day Washington and Lee University) in Lexington, Virginia. Acquainted with future Confederate general Thomas J. (Stonewall) Jackson, who taught at the nearby Virginia Military Institute, he married Isabella Sophia Morrison, the sister of

Jackson's second wife. Isabella was one of three daughters of the Reverend Robert Hall Morrison (president of Davidson College) who married Confederate generals. One daughter married Jackson, and another married Rufus Barringer. Apparently Hill's association with the Morrisons led him to leave Washington College and accept a position as professor of mathematics at Davidson College. He left that institution in 1859 to become superintendent, professor of mathematics, and artillery instructor at the North Carolina Military Institute at Charlotte.

With the outbreak of the Civil War, and on the eve of North Carolina's secession and alliance with the Confederacy, Governor John W. Ellis called on Hill to organize the first camp of instruction for North Carolina soldiers. He was elected colonel of the First Regiment North Carolina Volunteers on May 11, 1861. Several days later, North Carolina left the Union and joined the newly formed Confederate States of America.

Hill led his infantry regiment at the Battle of Big Bethel, south of Yorktown, Virginia, on June 10. In that action—the first significant fighting for Tar Heels in the war—his soldiers drove their Federal opponents from the field. He received promotion to brigadier general soon thereafter and transferred back to North Carolina to help improve the state's defenses.

Hill returned to Virginia in time to participate in the Peninsula Campaign (March–July 1862), in which a Confederate army commanded by General Joseph E. Johnston attempted to halt the advance toward Richmond of the U.S. Army of the Potomac, under the leadership of General George B. McClellan. Having been promoted to major general, with date of rank from March 26, Hill led a division in action at Williamsburg on May 26 and at the Battle of Seven Pines (May 31–June 1). Johnston was wounded in that battle, and General Robert E. Lee took his place in command of the Confederate troops defending against McClellan's assault. Lee subsequently reorganized his force into the Army of Northern Virginia. Under his leadership, Hill took his division into battle at Mechanicsville, Gaines Mill, and Malvern Hill (June 26–July 1). The last confrontation brought an end to McClellan's campaign and led to his withdrawal from the peninsula between the York and James Rivers.

In the next two months, Hill remained away from Virginia to command operations in North Carolina. He then returned to help supervise the buildup of defenses in the Richmond-Petersburg area, before rejoining the Army of Northern Virginia and resuming command of his division.

In the invasion of Maryland, which culminated in the Battle of Sharpsburg (or Antietam) on September 17, Hill and his division performed with skill and courage, although the general was unjustly accused of being responsible for the Confederate battle plan's accidentally falling into the hands of the Union army. At the battle, McClellan's Army of the Potomac forced Lee's retreat into Virginia. During the campaign, Hill skillfully delayed the Union advance at South Mountain on the fourteenth, and his soldiers stood fast in the vicious fighting at the Bloody Lane on the seventeenth.

When General Lee reorganized his army in October, he did not consider Hill for command of one of the corps. He was, according to Lee, "an excellent executive officer" but did not have "much administrative ability. Left to himself he seems embarrassed and backward to act." Because of his hurt feelings over not being given corps command and promotion to lieutenant general, as well as because of health problems, Hill threatened to resign from the army. But his brother-in-law, General Stonewall Jackson, convinced him to remain at his post.

Hill's effectiveness and advancement as a general were inhibited by his stubborn, irascible personality and his propensity to complain and criticize his superiors. His fellow officers and commanders did not question his courage but were alienated by his negativism and lack of cooperation. As a result, he found himself transferred on a number of occasions.

In early 1863, for example, he was placed under the command of General James Longstreet, in the Department of Virginia and North Carolina, and given the assignments of gathering supplies and attacking the Federal army occupying much of coastal North Carolina. His assaults on the Federal-held towns of New Bern and Washington in March and April proved largely unsuccessful.

In July, Lee's army suffered defeat by the Army of the Potomac, then led by General George G. Meade, at the Battle of Gettysburg. As the Army of Northern Virginia marched into Pennsylvania en route to its showdown at Gettysburg, Hill and his troops moved back into Virginia to defend Richmond. After Lee's devastating defeat and the retreat into Virginia, Hill returned to North Carolina. There he received temporary promotion to lieutenant general and orders to report to the western theater to command a corps in General Braxton Bragg's Army of Tennessee.

At the Battle of Chickamauga (September 19–20, 1863), Hill played a credible role in the victory over the U.S. Army of the Cumberland, commanded by General William Rosecrans. But his prickly nature led him into a quarrel with General Bragg, who was universally disliked by his chief officers. When those officers submitted a petition to President Jefferson Davis requesting Bragg's removal, the general blamed Hill. Instead of dismissing Bragg, Davis removed Hill from the Army of Tennessee—the only officer to be so withdrawn. The disagreement with Bragg also cost Hill a permanent promotion to lieutenant general. Davis, who considered Hill obnoxious, declined to send the recommendation to the Confederate Senate for approval.

After his dismissal from the western theater, Hill held only minor positions in the eastern campaigns. He served for a time as an aide to General Pierre G.T. Beauregard, commanded a division for a few days, and functioned as inspector general for the trenches in the Richmond-Petersburg area. He became commander of the District of Georgia in January 1865. He ended his career with General Joseph E. Johnston as Johnston held off the advance through the Carolinas of the army of General William T. Sherman in the final weeks of the war. Hill fought with Johnston against Sherman at the Battle of Bentonville, North Carolina (March 19–20, 1865), in which the U.S. forces triumphed. He was present at Johnston's surrender at the Bennett Farmhouse near Durham Station on April 26.

Following the war, Hill settled in Charlotte and published a monthly magazine, the *Land We Love*, from 1866 to 1869. He then began publishing a weekly newspaper, the *Southern Home*. He promoted education, especially technical or vocational training, for the state's impoverished population, a cause that would be taken up by his son, Daniel Harvey Hill Jr., an active educator and president of the North Carolina College of Agriculture and Mechanic Arts (present-day North Carolina State University) at Raleigh.

Hill left North Carolina to serve as president of the Arkansas Industrial University (the present University of Arkansas) from 1877 to 1884. He then assumed leadership of the Middle Georgia Military and Agricultural College at Milledgeville. He died of cancer in Charlotte on September 24, 1889, and was buried at the cemetery at Davidson College.

Hill never lived up to his potential as a Confederate general. Poor health might have been a factor. A spinal problem had given him pain since childhood, and he endured dysentery, piles, and various other maladies that at times left him absent from duty. But it was his quarrelsome personality that in the end hindered his military success.

John Franklin Hoke

1820–1888
State Adjutant General and Brigadier General of Militia

John Franklin Hoke was born in Lincolnton, North Carolina, on May 30, 1820. His family was of German descent and prominent in business and state politics. Robert F. Hoke, a major general in the Confederate army, was his nephew.

John F. Hoke graduated from Pleasant Retreat Academy in Lincoln County and then attended the University of North Carolina at Chapel Hill, graduating in 1841. He studied law under former governor and president of the university David L. Swain and with Richmond M. Pearson, chief justice of the North Carolina Supreme Court. Admitted to the bar, he practiced law in Lincolnton.

Hoke gained military experience during the Mexican-American War (1846–48), serving as a first lieutenant and then a captain in the U.S. forces fighting in Mexico. Following the war, he returned to the practice of law in North Carolina and became involved in state politics, serving in the state Senate in the 1850s and the House of Commons in 1860. He was a states' rights Democrat and a strong supporter of secession.

When North Carolina left the Union on May 20, 1861, and soon joined the Confederacy, Hoke was serving as state adjutant general with the rank of brigadier general. He helped organize several regiments of North Carolina troops for Confederate service in Virginia. But his tenure in that office and as a state-appointed brigadier general was short-lived. In July, he accepted a commission as colonel of the Twenty-third Regiment North Carolina Troops (originally designated the Thirteenth Regiment North Carolina Volunteers). That infantry unit arrived on the field too late to participate in the First Battle of Manassas (July 21) in Virginia.

But Hoke led his troops in combat during the Peninsula Campaign (March–July 1862), when the Confederate force, led first by General Joseph E. Johnston and then by General Robert E. Lee, opposed an advance on Richmond by the U.S. Army of the Potomac, commanded by General George B. McClellan. The Federals advanced toward the Confederate capital from the coast and along the peninsula between the York and James Rivers. In that campaign, Hoke saw action at a battle at Williamsburg on May 5.

Hoke's regiment was reorganized five days later, and he was not reelected colonel. He returned to Lincoln County, where he was soon elected to the state Senate. But his military career was not over. In August 1864, Hoke took command of the newly organized Fourth Regiment North Carolina Senior Reserves, a unit of overage soldiers with the duties of guarding prisoners, protecting certain sites, and hunting down deserters. The regiment helped guard Federal prisoners at the notorious Salisbury Prison and saw action only in a brief skirmish when some Union troops attempted to free detainees.

In the early days of postwar Reconstruction, Hoke served in the state House of Representatives as a member of the Conservative (later Democratic) Party. His officeholding, however, soon came to an end with the onset of Congressional (sometimes called Radical) Reconstruction, although he remained active in the Democratic Party for years. He continued to practice law and became involved in a number of business ventures, including a gold mine and railroad development. He served as a trustee of the University of North Carolina from 1874 to 1879 and as a vestryman in his Episcopal church. Hoke's wife, Catherine Alexander, died in 1857, and he never remarried. They had two daughters and a son, William A. Hoke, who became a state legislator and chief justice of the North Carolina Supreme Court.

While watching a political parade from his front porch in Lincolnton on October 27, 1888, Hoke suddenly fell dead. He was buried at the churchyard at St. Luke's Episcopal Church in that town.

Robert Frederick Hoke

1837–1912
Major General

Robert Frederick Hoke was born in Lincolnton on May 27, 1837. He attended Pleasant Retreat Academy in his hometown and then, in 1852, enrolled at the Kentucky Military Institute, near Frankfort. He returned home after one year to help manage the family business and manufacturing interests. He left North Carolina in 1860 and took a job at the U.S. Census Bureau in Washington, D.C. A Democrat and confirmed advocate of southern rights, he joined a group in Washington known as the Minute Men. Its purpose was to protect southern politicians, presumably from violence, amid the heated sectional discord that was fast propelling the nation toward disunion and war. Apparently, Hoke attended the inauguration of President Abraham Lincoln in March 1861.

On April 12, newly formed Confederate troops fired on the Federal-held Fort Sumter in the harbor of Charleston, South Carolina. President Lincoln then asked the states still in the Union for troops to suppress the rebellion. North Carolina refused the request and called for a Secession Convention, during which delegates passed an Ordinance of Secession on May 20. The state soon joined the other seceded states in the new Confederate States of America.

Hoke and other like-minded young men of Lincoln County, however, did not await their state's official secession before forming a military unit. On April 22, he and ninety-six others met in Lincolnton and organized an infantry company known as the Southern Stars. Hoke was elected second lieutenant. The company traveled by train to Raleigh, where at nearby Camp Ellis it joined other volunteer units to form the First Regiment North Carolina Volunteers, commanded by Colonel D.H. Hill. Hoke and his regiment took part in the small battle at Big Bethel Church, Virginia, in June.

In August, when the First North Carolina Volunteers mustered into the Confederate army, Hoke was elected major as Colonel Hill was promoted to brigadier general and transferred. The regiment continued service in Virginia until its six-month tour as a volunteer unit ended in November. Hoke then received an appointment as major in the Thirty-third Regiment North Carolina Troops, and after spending some time at home, he joined his new regiment in Raleigh in early January 1862.

The Thirty-third deployed to New Bern, North Carolina, to help defend the town against Federal attack. A U.S. expedition captured Roanoke Island in February, and in March it moved on New Bern. Following a victory over the Confederate defenders at the battle there, the U.S. Army would remain in control of much of coastal North Carolina for the rest of the war, with a headquarters in the town. Soon after the Thirty-third arrived in New Bern in January, its commander, Colonel Lawrence O'Bryan Branch, was promoted to brigadier general, and Lieutenant Colonel Clark M. Avery became colonel of the regiment. Hoke thus rose to lieutenant colonel and second in command. Overwhelmed in the Battle of New Bern on March 14, the Confederate forces withdrew from their defenses, and Avery was captured during the retreat. Hoke then took command of the regiment and led its flight westward to Kinston.

Hoke and his troops, along with the rest of Branch's brigade, embarked by train for Virginia on May 4. After a short encampment at Gordonsville, the brigade was ordered to reinforce General Thomas J. (Stonewall) Jackson in the Shenandoah Valley. But when Branch's men reached the foot of the Blue Ridge Mountains, they were suddenly ordered back to the Richmond area. There, along with other units of Branch's brigade, Hoke's regiment skirmished against Federal troops led by General Irvin McDowell at Slash Church. In early June, the brigade joined the division of General A.P. Hill in the corps of Stonewall Jackson.

During the subsequent Seven Days Battles (June 25–July 1), the newly formed Army of Northern Virginia, under the leadership of General Robert

E. Lee, drove the U.S. expedition of General George B. McClellan away from Richmond and back down the peninsula between the York and James Rivers. In that campaign, Hoke led the Thirty-third in battles at Gaines Mill and Frayser's Farm. Lee's assault ended at the Battle of Malvern Hill, where Hoke's troops came under bombardment from gunboats and land batteries but were not heavily engaged.

With the end of the Seven Days Battles and McClellan's march toward Richmond, the Thirty-third Regiment moved back to Gordonsville. Having proven his ability to command since the Battle of New Bern, Hoke received promotion to full colonel and permanent command of his regiment, with date of rank from August 5. Four days later, A.P. Hill's division marched quickly to support General Jackson at Cedar Mountain, where the Confederates confronted a corps of General John Pope's U.S. Army of Virginia. That action was a preliminary to the main Second Battle of Manassas (or Bull Run) on August 29–30. At Cedar Mountain, Hoke's troops help drive back a Federal advance, sustaining a loss of six killed and thirty wounded.

Following Cedar Mountain, Hoke's troops returned to the Gordonsville area, where they encamped. But they were soon on the move again and went into action at Second Manassas. In that struggle, Lee's Confederates dealt a sound defeat to Pope's force. When Lee subsequently invaded Maryland in early September, Hoke's regiment took part in Jackson's seizure of Harpers Ferry and then became engaged at Sharpsburg (or Antietam), where, on September 17, the Army of Northern Virginia fought a bloody battle with the Army of the Potomac, commanded by McClellan.

Repulsed at Sharpsburg, Lee retreated into Virginia, where Hoke's regiment went into camp for the autumn. During that time, Avery was released from the Union prison at Johnson's Island, Ohio, and again took command of the Thirty-third. Hoke was transferred to the command of the Twenty-first Regiment North Carolina Troops, in the brigade of General Isaac R. Trimble and the division of General Jubal A. Early. Hoke assumed command of the brigade in the absence of Trimble, who had been wounded in August at Second Manassas.

At the Battle of Fredericksburg in December, Lee's army from an impregnable position inflicted heavy losses on an attack ordered by General Ambrose E. Burnside and forced the Federals' retreat. For his leadership in repelling the attack on the Confederate right, Hoke received high praise from Early, who described him as "an officer of great energy and industry" who "displayed the most conspicuous gallantry…and the ability to command of a very high order." In that action, an accident of potentially serious results befell Hoke when his horse tumbled during an artillery barrage. Hoke also fell, and his foot became caught in the stirrup. The horse then ran, dragging Hoke. Stunned but not seriously injured, Hoke managed to recover quickly and remain in command.

He was not so lucky, however, at the subsequent Battle of Chancellorsville (May 1–4, 1863), where Lee scored another victory over the Army of the Potomac, this time led by General Joseph Hooker. Hoke had received promotion to brigadier general on April 23, with date of rank from January, and was in permanent command of Trimble's old brigade. He was severely wounded on May 4 when a minié ball struck him in the left shoulder. Surgeons operated the same day. He was out of action until late July 1863, when he returned to command of his brigade, then near Madison Court House, Virginia.

In September, he was detached from the brigade to take command of a special force and lead it to North Carolina to hunt down deserters and draft dodgers. Desertion of North Carolinians from Confederate ranks had reached epidemic proportions, and General Lee and Governor Zebulon B. Vance had insisted that efforts be made to check it. Hoke encountered his greatest difficulties in the Quaker Belt counties of the Piedmont as he hunted for outliers who had deserted or evaded conscription. In cooperation with the Home Guard, his troops ambushed, captured, and killed a number of deserters and draft dodgers. But their efforts brought only marginal success.

In late January 1864, Hoke, who had returned to Virginia and rejoined his brigade, led his men back to North Carolina to participate in General George Pickett's attempt to recapture New Bern from the Federals. Pickett's attack having failed, President Jefferson Davis ordered Hoke and his brigade to encamp near Raleigh. A sizable peace movement had arisen in North Carolina, led by Raleigh newspaper editor William W. Holden, who announced his plans to run against the incumbent governor, Zebulon B. Vance, in the upcoming election. Davis considered having Hoke arrest Holden and retain him under a recent law suspending habeas corpus. Vance, however, convinced the president not to have Holden arrested. The editor temporarily suspended publication of his newspaper, the *North Carolina Standard*, and his clamor against the Confederate government.

In March, Hoke received orders to replace Pickett in command of Confederate forces in eastern North Carolina. It was there, at the Battle of Plymouth in April, that he was to achieve his greatest success during the war.

Hoke considered the recapture of Plymouth, occupied by a U.S. force under the command of General Henry W. Wessells, to be the first step in forcing the Union army from coastal North Carolina. Located on Albemarle Sound, the town provided a base for control of that body of water and served as a supply center for the Federals. Skillfully planning and launching his attack, Hoke effected the surrender of the U.S. garrison on the morning of April 20. His assault was assisted in large measure by the ironclad CSS *Albemarle*, which steamed down from its berth on the Roanoke River to overwhelm the Union fleet and bombard the local defenses.

In the final throes of the battle, the Tar Heel general's men massacred a large number of African American Union soldiers, summarily executing those who tried to surrender and chasing others into the swamps, where they shot them in cold blood. Black women and children captured at Plymouth were remanded into slavery. According to Hoke's biographer, however, "No evidence has ever been discovered that would suggest Hoke either ordered, knew about, or acquiesced in the incident." Upon learning of the victory at Plymouth, President Davis sent Hoke words of praise and congratulations and the news that he had been promoted to major general.

After his success at Plymouth, Hoke launched an attack on the Union stronghold at New Bern. His troops were only one day into their assault, however, when General Lee ordered him to withdraw and move his force back to the Petersburg-Richmond area to help hold off a Federal advance. The transfer of the North Carolinian's soldiers to Virginia in early May ended attempts by the Confederacy to recapture coastal North Carolina from the Yankee occupiers.

In May, Hoke's division fought at the Battle of Drewry's Bluff. There Confederates under overall command of General Pierre G.T. Beauregard forced the withdrawal of Federals led by General Benjamin F. Butler onto the neck of Bermuda Hundred, a peninsula between the James and Appomattox Rivers. Locked in that position, Butler's force was unable to maneuver for the rest of the war.

As the month drew to a close, Hoke shifted his division to Cold Harbor, where a tremendous battle ensued between Lee's army and the Army of the Potomac, led by General in Chief Ulysses S. Grant and tactical commander General George G. Meade. Grant's overall objectives were to apply unrelenting pressure on Lee, drive him back toward Richmond, and force his surrender. The Confederates inflicted heavy casualties on the Federals at Cold Harbor, where Hoke's troops held "a position vital to the successful strategy of Robert E. Lee."

Undeterred by his losses, however, Grant flanked Lee and drove toward the Confederate capital from the south. The Confederates managed to get in front of his advance, and the two armies went into trenches around besieged Petersburg. Hoke's division remained in those defensive works until late December 1864, when it transferred to Wilmington, North Carolina, to help protect that blockade-running port and Fort Fisher, the town's chief defense, from a joint Union army and navy assault.

On January 15, 1865, a U.S. assault led by General Alfred H. Terry and Admiral David D. Porter captured Fort Fisher, which was commanded by Colonel William Lamb. Hoke's troops might have played a significant role in repelling the Federal attack if General Braxton Bragg, in charge of the overall defenses at Wilmington, had utilized them effectively. But Bragg apparently misjudged the situation and failed to respond with reinforcements or decisive action. After the fall of Fort Fisher and the Federal occupation of Wilmington, blockade-running ended for the Confederacy.

Bragg then retreated northwestward, pursued by the force of General Jacob D. Cox. General John M. Schofield at New Bern had ordered Cox to press the Confederates as they withdrew. In the fighting around Kinston, especially at Southwest Creek, Hoke led his soldiers in effective rearguard actions. At the subsequent Battle of Bentonville, Hoke's troops, which then included boys of the North Carolina Junior Reserves, fought fiercely on March 19 and 20. That battle, a defeat for the Confederates, was the last major effort by General Joseph E. Johnston's army to halt the advance of the army of General William T. Sherman into North Carolina. When Johnston formally surrendered to Sherman in late April at the Bennett Farmhouse in present-day Durham, Hoke's division was in northern Randolph County. Johnston's surrender ended the Civil War, Lee having surrendered to Grant at Appomattox Court House, Virginia, some days earlier.

After the war, Hoke became involved in a number of business and mining ventures and served as a director of the North Carolina Railroad. In 1869, he married Lydia Ann Wyck, a native of Pendleton, South Carolina, who had attended school in Raleigh and visited Lincolnton. The couple settled in Raleigh and had six children, the last of whom died at the age of six months. Hoke died of complications from diabetes in Lincolnton on July 3, 1912. He was buried at Raleigh's Oakwood Cemetery.

Theophilus Hunter Holmes

1804–1880
Lieutenant General

Theophilus Hunter Holmes was born in Sampson County, North Carolina, on November 13, 1804, the son of Gabriel and Mary Hunter Holmes. His father served as governor of the state from 1821 to 1824. Holmes entered the U.S. Military Academy at West Point in 1825 and graduated four years later.

As a U.S. infantry officer, he served on the frontier and in a campaign against the Seminoles in Florida, receiving promotion to captain in 1838. In the Mexican-American War (1846–48), he led a charge at the siege of Monterrey and was awarded the brevet rank of major. That became a

permanent promotion in the Eighth U.S. Infantry in 1855, and Holmes saw duty mainly in the West before taking command of the army's recruiting service, with a headquarters on Governors Island, New York.

With the outbreak of the Civil War in April 1861, Holmes became one of fifteen U.S. Army field-grade officers to resign their commissions and join the Confederate army. Some friends and fellow officers tried to persuade him to reconsider his decision to leave the Federal army. They proposed obtaining a leave of absence that would allow him to live in Europe until the pending war ended, thereby relieving him of the dilemma and pain of fighting against his Southern homeland. Holmes, however, declined and returned to North Carolina to assist in organizing the state's troops for service in Confederate ranks. Governor Henry T. Clark appointed him commander of the Southern Department of North Carolina's coastal region, to establish defenses against Federal invasion of the area from Onslow County down to the South Carolina line.

On June 5, 1861, President Jefferson Davis, Holmes's West Point classmate, appointed him brigadier general in the Confederate army. He commanded a reserve brigade at the First Battle of Manassas (or Bull Run) in Virginia in July. In that struggle, the Confederates, commanded by General Pierre G.T. Beauregard, won a victory over the Union army led by General Irvin McDowell. Holmes's brigade did not take part in the fighting. Nevertheless, he received promotion to major general on October 7, 1861. He continued to lead troops in Virginia until March 1862, when he was assigned to command the Department of North Carolina and oversee the defense of the eastern part of the state. There he "did creditably in reorganizing the defenses" but "may not have been aggressive" in thwarting Federal attacks.

Holmes returned to Virginia to command a division in the Seven Days Battles (June 25–July 1). In that campaign, the newly created Army of Northern Virginia, led by General Robert E. Lee, halted the Union advance toward Richmond commanded by General George B. McClellan and drove the Federals from the peninsula between the James and York Rivers. At the Battle of Malvern Hill (July 1), the last of the Seven Days encounters, Holmes's division was present, but he "allowed the day to pass and the battle to be decided in his hearing without doing more than forming his men in line of battle."

Shortly thereafter, President Davis appointed him commander of the Trans-Mississippi Department, with headquarters at Little Rock, Arkansas. In October, Davis promoted him to lieutenant general. Holmes at first declined the promotion and then reluctantly accepted it. In the next two months, a Federal army commanded by General Ulysses S. Grant threatened the Confederate stronghold at Vicksburg on the Mississippi River. The War Department ordered Holmes to send troops to aid in opposing Grant's advance. He refused, however, arguing that to transfer them across the river would lead to the capture and occupation of Arkansas by Union forces. Then the Confederates suffered defeats at Prairie Grove, Arkansas, on December 7, 1862, and Arkansas Post on January 11, 1863. As a result of those losses, as well as Holmes's disobedience of orders about reinforcing Vicksburg, Davis removed him from command of the Trans-Mississippi Department and gave that position to General Edmund Kirby Smith. The president then assigned Holmes to the command of the District of Arkansas.

In June 1863, General Kirby Smith ordered Holmes to capture the Federal garrison at Helena, Arkansas, in an effort to relieve Vicksburg, then under siege by Grant. But Holmes's attack was poorly coordinated and was repelled, with a loss of more than 1,600 men. Apparently despondent over his failure, Holmes is said to have "vainly sought death on the battlefield." He then was confined to bed with a severe headache, refusing to have visitors and unable to conduct business. General Sterling Price took command of the district temporarily and retreated from Little Rock to southern Arkansas. In late September, Holmes had recovered sufficiently to resume responsibility for the district. But the following January, General Kirby Smith requested that Holmes be replaced by a younger man, remarking that the North Carolinian's memory seemed to be failing. Learning of Kirby Smith's request, Holmes resigned from his Arkansas post. The War Department then ordered him to report to Richmond.

From the Confederate capital, he was again assigned to North Carolina, this time to command reserve troops. On September 16, 1864, he was admitted to the general hospital at Wilmington. No diagnosis has survived, but apparently he had recovered by December and resumed leading troops in the area in the final days before Fort Fisher and the port of Wilmington fell to U.S. Navy and Army attack.

After the war, Holmes settled on a small farm near Fayetteville. He died on June 21, 1880. As he requested, he was buried in a soldier's coffin in the cemetery at MacPherson Presbyterian Church in Fayetteville. He had married Laura Wetmore of North Carolina in 1841, but she had died while he was on U.S. recruiting duty in New York in 1859. The couple had six children.

Although described by one observer as "a splendid example of an unpretentious North Carolina patriot and gentleman," Holmes apparently did not live up to the level of leadership required of a general officer. His performance was marginal at best, and he was frequently criticized by other generals. He might have owed his high rank as lieutenant general, at least in part, to his friendship with President Jefferson Davis. His performance might have been hindered to some extent by physical or mental ailments in times of stress. He might even have suffered from temporary deafness on the battlefield when he was reported to be "totally unaware of extremely loud gunfire." In any event, he was among a number of prewar U.S. Army officers—and West Point graduates—who did not measure up to expectations as Civil War generals.

Alfred Iverson Jr.

1829–1911
Brigadier General

A lfred Iverson Jr. was not a native North Carolinian, but he commanded North Carolina troops and had ancestral ties to the Tar Heel State. He was born in Jones County, Georgia, on February 14, 1829, and at times has been confused with his father, Senator Alfred Iverson, who was a strong advocate for southern rights.

At age seventeen, the younger Iverson began his military career as a second lieutenant in a Georgia volunteer regiment, having attended Tuskegee Military Institute in Alabama. He saw action in the Mexican-American War (1846–48) and then returned to civilian life to study law briefly and work as a railroad contractor. In 1855, he acquired a commission in the regular U.S. Army as a first lieutenant in the First U.S. Cavalry and served in Kansas, Utah, and the Indian Territory. With the outbreak of the Civil War, he resigned from the Federal army and returned to Georgia, where he was commissioned a captain in the Confederate army.

Iverson soon received orders to report to General Theophilus H. Holmes at Wilmington, North Carolina, to help in establishing the state's coastal defenses. He commanded troops at the mouth of the Cape Fear River until the Twentieth Regiment North Carolina Troops (originally designated the

Alfred Iverson Jr.

Tenth Regiment North Carolina Volunteers) was formed on June 18, 1861. He helped organize and then became colonel of that infantry regiment. All its other officers and men were North Carolinians.

The Twentieth Regiment saw action in Virginia during the Seven Days Battles (June 25–July 1), when General Robert E. Lee led his Army of Northern Virginia in a counterattack to drive the U.S. Army of the Potomac, led by General George B. McClellan, away from Richmond and off the peninsula between the York and James Rivers. Iverson's regiment, along with four others from North Carolina, formed part of the brigade of General Samuel Garland of Virginia and the division of General D.H. Hill.

On June 27, 1862, during the Battle of Gaines Mill, the Twentieth assaulted a Federal artillery position near a swamp in the vicinity of Cold Harbor. Historian Douglas Southall Freeman described the attack:

> *The Twentieth North Carolina, under a former regular, Col. Alfred Iverson, maneuvered separately into position to deliver an independent assault. As this regiment came into the open, the Division held its breath. Iverson fell, but Lt. Col. Franklin J. Faison took his place. A few minutes more, and the Carolinians were in full cry; a little longer and they were upon the guns. The instant Hill saw his men struggling with the Federal artillerists, he unloosed every regiment on the southern edge of the swamp. In a long, cheering line, they mounted the ridge. Soon the Federals were wavering, were breaking.*

Although Iverson's troops did not hold the captured guns, General Hill, known for his critical nature, declared that "no doubt a greater loss was saved to the Division in its advance by this gallant attack."

Iverson's wound evidently was serious, and he spent some time recovering but was back at the head of his regiment by the time the Army of Northern Virginia invaded Maryland in September. When a portion of General Lee's troops clashed with those of McClellan at South Mountain on September 14, Iverson and his regiment, along with the Thirteenth North Carolina, were "furiously assailed on the left" of the battle line, but they "received the assault calmly." General Garland fell mortally wounded at South Mountain, and Colonel Duncan K. McRae of the Fifth Regiment North Carolina State Troops took command of the brigade.

Iverson led his regiment in the subsequent and bloody Battle of Sharpsburg (or Antietam) on September 17. The entire brigade sustained heavy losses in the infamous Cornfield. Halted by McClellan's army at that battle, General Lee withdrew his force into Virginia. On November 1, Iverson received promotion to brigadier general and permanent command of Garland's old brigade, replacing McRae, who was passed over for promotion and resigned from the army.

At the Battle of Fredericksburg in December, Lee's army devastated the Union ranks during an ill-conceived attack by the Army of the Potomac, then led by General Ambrose E. Burnside. Iverson's brigade saw little action there, although it endured heavy artillery fire. In early May 1863, his brigade participated in the Battle of Chancellorsville, in which the Army of Northern Virginia again triumphed over the Army of the Potomac, this time led by General Joseph Hooker. On the third day of the battle, Iverson suffered a "contusion in the groin from a spent shell, which made walking very painful."

Iverson's career and reputation received a severe blow when General Lee marched his army into Pennsylvania and came to grips again with the Army of the Potomac, then commanded by General George G. Meade. On the first day of the Battle of Gettysburg (July 1–3, 1863), the U.S. First Corps virtually wiped out Iverson's brigade. Apparently the disaster resulted at least partly from his error in judgment. The Federal soldiers ambushed Iverson's troops from behind a stone wall and simultaneously struck the regiment's front and flanks. Having seen most of his men killed, wounded, or captured, Iverson "went to pieces." He managed to collect himself enough to assist ably in the Confederate retreat to Virginia following the Federal victory at Gettysburg. But his failure at that battle had tarnished his reputation as a leader, and he was soon exiled from the Virginia campaigns.

Iverson received orders to report to his home state of Georgia, where he was to recruit and command state troops. As the U.S. Army led by General William T. Sherman threatened that state from the northwest, Iverson had a chance to redeem his reputation in defense of Georgia and its major city, Atlanta. He was assigned a brigade in the cavalry corps of General Joseph Wheeler in February 1864. Near Macon on July 27, his brigade captured General George Stoneman and several hundred horse soldiers. That action is considered one of the most successful cavalry operations of the war, although four days later, Iverson was reported sick and not on duty.

Sherman's army took Atlanta on September 1, 1864, captured Savannah in December, and then marched northward through the Carolinas. The war ended for Iverson and the Confederacy when General Joseph E. Johnston surrendered to Sherman at the Bennett Farmhouse near Durham Station, North Carolina, in April 1865.

Alfred Iverson Jr.

After the war, Iverson went into business in Macon. In 1877, he moved to Florida and became an orange grower. Later, he returned to Atlanta to live with his daughter's family. He died in that city on March 31, 1911, and was buried there at Oakland Cemetery. Iverson was married twice—once to Harriet Harris Hutchins, with whom he had two daughters, and then to Adela Branham.

Robert Daniel Johnston

1837–1919
Brigadier General

Robert Daniel Johnston was born at Mount Welcome in Lincoln County, North Carolina, on March 19, 1837. He graduated from the University of North Carolina at Chapel Hill in 1858 and then studied law at the University of Virginia. Returning to North Carolina, he became a member of the bar and practiced law. He was an officer in the Lincoln County Militia when his native state seceded and embraced the Confederacy. He joined the Confederate army as a captain of Company K, Twenty-third Regiment North Carolina Troops (originally designated the Thirteenth Regiment North Carolina Volunteers). Four brothers of Johnston also served in that regiment.

The Twenty-third fought in the Peninsula Campaign (March–July 1862) in Virginia, in which a Confederate army, first commanded by General Joseph E. Johnston, opposed an assault by the U.S. Army of the Potomac, led by General George B. McClellan. The Federal force threatened the Confederate capital at Richmond via the peninsula between the York and James Rivers. On May 10, Robert Daniel Johnston received a promotion to lieutenant colonel and became second in command of his regiment. At the Battle of Seven Pines (Fair Oaks) on May 31, he was wounded in the arm and upper body, and his horse was killed under him. He convalesced and returned to duty in September. General Johnston had also been wounded at Seven Pines, and General Robert E. Lee took his place at the head of the Confederate forces in Virginia, reorganizing them into the Army of Northern Virginia, which he led until the war's conclusion.

Robert Daniel Johnston rejoined his regiment just in time to accompany it and the Army of Northern Virginia on the invasion of Maryland, where the Confederates clashed with General McClellan's Army of the Potomac at South Mountain and at the horrendous Battle of Sharpsburg (or Antietam). On September 17 at Sharpsburg, the Twenty-third, in General Samuel Garland's brigade and General D.H. Hill's division, held the center of the Confederate line at the famous sunken road known as the Bloody Lane. For Johnston's leadership and courage in the fighting, Hill referred to him as "the gallant lieutenant colonel." Ultimately repulsed by McClellan's forces, Lee's army retreated into Virginia.

At the subsequent Battle of Chancellorsville (May 1–4, 1863), the Army of Northern Virginia won a decisive victory over the Army of the Potomac, this time led by General Joseph Hooker. In that encounter, Johnston temporarily commanded the Twelfth Regiment North Carolina Troops (originally designated the Second Regiment North Carolina Volunteers) following the death of its senior officer. That regiment was part of the division of General Robert E. Rodes, who had replaced D.H. Hill, and the Second Corps of General Thomas J. (Stonewall) Jackson. On May 12, the Twelfth Regiment took part in Jackson's flanking maneuver that turned the tide of the battle and brought the Confederates a decisive victory. Johnston's troops fought hard and captured a stand of the enemy's colors. Unfortunately for Lee and his army, Jackson was accidentally killed by his own troops during the battle. General Richard S. Ewell replaced him as leader of the Second Corps. Johnston soon returned to his old regiment, the Twenty-third.

After his victory at Chancellorsville, Lee marched his army into Pennsylvania, where it fought against the Army of the Potomac, then led by General George G. Meade, at the Battle of Gettysburg (July 1–3, 1863). During the first day of the battle, Johnston was slightly wounded. The Confederate force suffered a resounding defeat and fled back to Virginia. In the retreat, Johnston was captured by Federal cavalry but was soon rescued by Confederate horsemen. On September 1, he was promoted to brigadier general and given command of the former brigade of General Alfred Iverson Jr.

In early May 1864, General Ulysses S. Grant, general in chief of the U.S. Army, began driving the Army of the Potomac, with Meade in tactical command, in his Overland Campaign to flank and force the surrender of the Army of Northern Virginia near Richmond. Although the Federals sustained high casualties at the Battles of the Wilderness (May 5–6), Spotsylvania Court House (May 7–19), and Cold Harbor (June 1–3), they ultimately forced Lee's army into entrenchments at Petersburg. At the Battle of Spotsylvania Court House, Johnston had led his troops on May 12 in planting a regimental flag on Federal works when he was wounded in the head and tumbled from his horse. He was hospitalized in a general hospital in Charlotte, North Carolina.

Johnston returned to action to lead his brigade, in the corps of General Jubal A. Early, who had replaced Ewell, in the Shenandoah Valley Campaign (August 7, 1864–March 2, 1865). In that campaign, Early scored a number of victories and even threatened the capital at Washington before ultimately being defeated by General Philip H. Sheridan and the U.S. Army of the Shenandoah. Johnston distinguished himself in fighting near Winchester in September 1864. He and his troops then served for a time in the trenches around Petersburg, where Grant's troops ultimately penetrated the defenses of the Army of Northern Virginia and forced its surrender at Appomattox Court House on April 9, 1865. But Johnston was not at that surrender. In March 1865, he and his soldiers had been assigned to northeastern North Carolina to guard the Roanoke River area and round up deserters. The war ended there for him, and he was paroled at Charlotte in May.

For the next two decades, Johnston practiced law in Charlotte. He then moved to Birmingham, Alabama, and became president of the Birmingham National Bank. He also practiced law and invested in business and mining operations in that city. He served as registrar of the Federal Land Bank Office for some years, and he and his wife helped found a state industrial school for boys near Birmingham. He had married Elizabeth Johnston Evans in 1871, and they had seven children. He died at the home of a son in Winchester, Virginia, on February 1, 1919, and was buried in that town.

William Whedbee Kirkland

1833–1915
Brigadier General

William Whedbee Kirkland was born at Ayr Mount, the family home near Hillsborough, North Carolina, on February 13, 1833. He attended the U.S. Military Academy at West Point but was expelled in 1855 for what he referred to with regret as "my improper course." He accepted a commission as second lieutenant in the U.S. Marine Corps that same year and saw service in China, but he resigned in 1860.

North Carolina seceded from the Union and joined the Confederate States of America in late May 1861. In the following month, the Twenty-first Regiment North Carolina Troops (originally designated the Eleventh Regiment North Carolina Volunteers) was formed, and Kirkland was elected its colonel. The infantry regiment soon moved to Virginia to join the Confederate force of General Pierre G.T. Beauregard. In July, Beauregard's troops defeated the Federal army of General Irvin McDowell at the First Battle of Manassas (or Bull Run). During that fighting, Kirkland's regiment was assigned to the brigade of General Milledge L. Bonham, which guarded the Confederate right flank and was not heavily engaged.

In October 1861, the Twenty-first North Carolina joined the brigade of General Isaac Trimble in the division of General Richard S. Ewell, which was under the overall command (in the Second Corps of the Army of Northern Virginia, as of October 1862) of the famed General Thomas J. (Stonewall) Jackson. When Jackson's force outmaneuvered and defeated the troops of General Nathaniel Banks in the Shenandoah Valley Campaign of May–June 1862, Kirkland led his regiment in attack at the First Battle of Winchester on May 25. In a charge to dislodge the Federal defenses formed behind a stone wall, Kirkland was seriously wounded in both thighs and taken from the battlefield on a stretcher. He spent a year recuperating, during which time he managed to serve temporarily on the staff of General Patrick R. Cleburne in Tennessee.

Kirkland rejoined his regiment in time to participate in the invasion of Pennsylvania by General Robert E. Lee's Army of Northern Virginia. At the ensuing Battle of Gettysburg (July 1–3, 1863), Lee's troops came to blows with the Army of the Potomac, commanded by General George G. Meade. On July 2, the Twenty-first took part in the famed and disastrous Confederate charge against the Federals holding Cemetery Ridge, which devastated Lee's army and led to its retreat into Virginia. In late August, Kirkland was promoted to brigadier general and placed in charge of the brigade of General James Johnston Pettigrew, who had been killed in the retreat from Gettysburg.

When elements of Lee's and Meade's armies again clashed at the Battle of Bristoe Station, Virginia, on October 14, Kirkland's brigade blundered into a Federal ambush and suffered the loss of 602 men, half of whom were captured. Again Kirkland was seriously wounded. A bullet fractured the ulna of his left arm. He was first placed in a recovery hospital in Gordonsville and was then transferred to a general hospital in Richmond, where he underwent surgery of some type before relocating to Savannah, Georgia, to recuperate.

He returned to duty in late February 1864 and took part in the Army of Northern Virginia's efforts to thwart the relentless assault of the Army of the Potomac, then led by the U.S. general in chief, Ulysses S. Grant, with Meade in tactical command. Grant's plan was to apply unceasing pressure on Lee's army, force it back toward Richmond, and secure its ultimate surrender. During the tremendous fighting that ensued, Kirkland's brigade suffered major losses at the Battle of the Wilderness (May 5–6). His men also fought at the Battle of Spotsylvania Court House and then at Cold Harbor, where on June 2 he was wounded again. A sharpshooter's bullet struck him in the right thigh, and he was admitted to Jackson Hospital in Richmond.

By August, Kirkland had recovered sufficiently to take command of the former brigade of General James G. Martin, in the division of General Robert F. Hoke. His troops took up a position north of the James River as the

Army of the Potomac besieged Lee's army in trenches around Petersburg. His brigade then accompanied Hoke's command when it was dispatched to North Carolina to help defend the port of Wilmington, protected by the formidable Fort Fisher. The brigade saw some skirmish action during a futile Federal attack by General Benjamin F. Butler and Admiral David D. Porter on December 24. Another assault, this time led by Porter and General Alfred H. Terry, captured the fort on January 15, 1865. Hoke's troops—especially Kirkland's brigade—might have been more effective in the defense of the fort if General Braxton Bragg, in overall command at Wilmington, had used them effectively. After the fall of Fort Fisher and the Federal occupation of Wilmington, blockade-running ended for the Confederacy.

Bragg withdrew his force northwestward into the interior of North Carolina, and he was pursued by General Jacob D. Cox, ordered by General John M. Schofield at New Bern to press the Confederates as they retreated. At the Battle of Wise's Forks near Kinston on March 8, Kirkland's men took part in Hoke's attack on Union lines, which captured a number of prisoners. Two days later, however, another Kirkland attack on well-entrenched Union lines proved unsuccessful and costly.

The last fighting for Kirkland and his troops came at the Battle of Bentonville on March 19–20, in which the Confederate force commanded by General Joseph E. Johnston attempted to halt the advance of the army of General William T. Sherman into North Carolina. When Johnston first heard heavy firing at the front, he inquired who had engaged the enemy. When told that it was Kirkland, he reportedly replied: "I am glad of it. I would rather they would attack Kirkland than any one else." Sherman triumphed at Bentonville and continued his march until Johnston surrendered to him at the Bennett Farmhouse, near Durham Station, on April 26, 1865, for all practical purposes ending the war.

Kirkland received his parole near Greensboro on May 1. He settled in Savannah, Georgia, and operated a commission business. He subsequently moved to New York and worked for the U.S. Post Office. Near the end of his life, he became an invalid and spent his last years in a soldiers' home in Washington, D.C. He died on May 12, 1915, and was buried in his son-in-law's family plot at Elmwood Cemetery near Shepherdstown, West Virginia.

Kirkland had married Susan A. Hardee before the war. She was the niece of General William J. Hardee, author of a manual on military tactics and Confederate corps commander in the Army of Tennessee. Their daughter, Elizabeth (Bess), gained fame on the Broadway stage using the name Odette Tyler.

James Henry Lane

1833–1907
Brigadier General

James Henry Lane was born at Matthews Court House, Virginia, on July 28, 1833. He received his education from private tutors and schools until 1851, when he entered the Virginia Military Institute at Lexington. After his 1854 graduation, as second in his class, he attended the University of Virginia, receiving a degree in science in 1857. He worked as an engineer on a hydrographic survey of the York River before accepting a position as professor of mathematics and military tactics instructor at the Virginia Military Institute. He left to become commandant and professor of mathematics at the State

Seminary of Florida. That appointment was followed by one as professor of natural philosophy and instructor of tactics at the North Carolina Military Institute in Charlotte, which was under the supervision of future Confederate general D.H. Hill.

At the outbreak of the Civil War and on the eve of North Carolina's secession and alliance with the new Confederate States of America, Governor John W. Ellis summoned Hill to Raleigh to organize the first camp of instruction for North Carolina soldiers. Lane, too, answered the call and assumed duties as adjutant and instructor of tactics at the camp. When the First Regiment North Carolina Volunteers was formed on May 11, 1861, Hill was elected colonel and Lane major. Several days later, North Carolina seceded from the Union and joined the Confederacy.

Lane's regiment soon transferred to Virginia, where it fought in the Battle of Big Bethel, south of Yorktown, on June 10, 1861. That was the first major fighting for Tar Heels in the war, and the men of the First Regiment forced the retreat of their Federal opponents. After the battle, Hill was promoted to brigadier general and sent back to North Carolina to help bolster the state's defenses. Lane then rose to lieutenant colonel and second in command of the regiment.

With a reorganization of North Carolina troops, Lane became colonel of the Twenty-eighth Regiment North Carolina Troops, in the brigade of General Lawrence O'Bryan Branch. That brigade also contained the Seventh, Eighteenth, Thirty-third, and Thirty-seventh Regiments North Carolina Troops. The brigade fought in the Peninsula Campaign (March–July 1862), in which the Confederates, commanded by General Joseph E. Johnston, opposed the U.S. Army of the Potomac, led by General George B. McClellan, as the Federals advanced from the coast toward Richmond along the peninsula between the York and James Rivers. The brigade went into action at Hanover Court House on May 27, where it sustained a significant number of casualties and was forced to retreat.

After General Johnston was wounded at the Battle of Seven Pines on May 31, General Robert E. Lee took his place and reorganized the Confederate units into the Army of Northern Virginia. At that time, Branch's brigade, which had been operating independently, joined the Light Division of General A.P. Hill. It took part in the ensuing Seven Days Battles (June 25–July 1), in which Lee drove McClellan from the peninsula in a series of bloody encounters. At Cold Harbor on June 27, Lane suffered a slight head wound. Three days later, at the Battle of Frayser's Farm (or White Oak Swamp), he received a flesh wound in the right cheek but did not leave the battlefield. Lee's counterattack against McClellan ended with the Battle of Malvern Hill, during which Lane's troops were held in reserve.

Lane and his men next saw major action at the Battle of Cedar Mountain on August 9 and the Second Battle of Manassas (or Bull Run) on August 29–30. In both encounters, the Army of Northern Virginia defeated the newly formed U.S. Army of Virginia, commanded by General John Pope. By that time, A.P. Hill's division was under the overall (eventually corps) command of General Thomas J. (Stonewall) Jackson.

When the Army of Northern Virginia invaded Maryland in mid-September, Lane's troops assisted in the capture of Harpers Ferry. At the Battle of Sharpsburg (or Antietam) on September 17, the Confederates were repulsed by McClellan's Army of the Potomac and were forced to flee back to Virginia. During the battle, Branch was killed, and command of his brigade passed to Lane, who skillfully led the troops as a rear guard for Lee's army as it retreated from Sharpsburg. His promotion to brigadier general became official on November 1.

At the Battle of Fredericksburg on December 13, Lee's Confederates crushed an ill-conceived attack by the Army of the Potomac, then commanded by General Ambrose E. Burnside. Lane's brigade occupied a position on the right of the Confederate line and in the middle of A.P. Hill's position. A gap in the alignment of Hill's brigades, however, allowed a Federal attack to break through temporarily and bring heavy losses on both sides. Lane's Twenty-eighth and Thirty-seventh Regiments bore the full force of the attack. Major William Morris of the Thirty-seventh recalled that the action was "the hardest fight I have ever been in…the Enemy advanced on us & we had to use the bayonet & butts of our guns." But in the end, Lane's regiments reformed, the assault was repulsed, and the Battle of Fredericksburg proved an overwhelming victory for the Confederates.

That success was followed by another at the Battle of Chancellorsville (May 1–3, 1863), sometimes called Lee's masterpiece. The Confederates routed the troops of the Army of the Potomac, this time led by General Joseph Hooker, and Lane's brigade played a significant role. Unfortunately for the brigade's reputation, however, its Eighteenth Regiment, commanded by Colonel John D. Barry, fired the volley that accidentally mortally wounded Stonewall Jackson, whose death was a major blow to the Army of Northern Virginia. Following Jackson's demise, Lee reorganized his army, promoting A.P. Hill and placing him in charge of the Third Corps. Lane's brigade then became part of General William Dorsey Pender's division.

Hoping to build on his recent victories, Lee invaded Pennsylvania in late June. His army became locked in battle again with the Army of the Potomac, then led by General George G. Meade, at the Battle of Gettysburg on July 1–3. When Pender was wounded on the second day, Lane temporarily commanded the division, but Lee quickly appointed General Isaac Trimble over him. Trimble's division was part of the famed and disastrous Confederate charge against the formidable Federal line on Cemetery Ridge on July 3. When Trimble fell wounded at the outset of the attack, Lane took charge of the division and led it in the assault. During the battle, his horse was shot from under him, but he continued to lead his troops until forced to retreat. The entire ill-fated attack failed and resulted in the virtual destruction of some Confederate units. Lane's brigade suffered 50 percent casualties. He would later claim that his soldiers were the last to withdraw from the field.

Having suffered a major defeat at Gettysburg, the Army of Northern Virginia fled back to Virginia. Again on home ground, Lane's brigade, along with the rest of Hill's corps, encamped in early August at Orange Court House, where the entire force would remain for nearly three months, resting and refurbishing. Despite sickness among the immobile soldiers, morale generally improved after the Gettysburg defeat and arduous retreat. But desertion was on the rise in the Army of Northern Virginia, and Lee ordered nine deserters in Lane's brigade shot by firing squad in September. After Pender's death from his Gettysburg wound, Lane was again passed over for division command, which went instead to General Cadmus M. Wilcox, another North Carolinian.

In May and June 1864, the Army of the Potomac and the Army of Northern Virginia fought in three horrendous Virginia battles that resulted in heavy casualties, especially for the attacking Federals. The Battle of the Wilderness, the Battle of Spotsylvania Court House, and the Battle of Cold Harbor all occurred as General Ulysses S. Grant, general in chief of the U.S. Army, led the Army of the Potomac, with Meade in tactical command, in the relentless Overland Campaign to press Lee's army toward Richmond and force its surrender. Lane's troops fought in all three encounters, playing a strong role in halting the Federal breakthrough at the famed Bloody Angle at Spotsylvania.

During an advance at Cold Harbor on June 2, a sharpshooter wounded Lane in the groin. He spent a period recuperating in Richmond and returned to his brigade on August 29. By that time, Grant and Meade had besieged Lee in the trenches around Petersburg. Lane again took medical leave on October 30 but had returned to Petersburg by February 1865. He continued to serve in that area as Lee's defenses and ranks dissolved in the final months of the war. Lane and the remnants of his brigade were with the Army of Northern Virginia when Lee surrendered to Grant at Appomattox Court House on April 9.

Following the war, Lane returned to the home of his parents in Virginia, where he found them destitute and grieving over the death of two sons who had fought with him. He then took employment teaching at private schools in Richmond and at Concord and Wilmington in North Carolina.

In 1869, he married Charlotte Randolph Meade of Richmond, with whom he had four daughters. His prospects improved when he became professor of natural philosophy and commandant at the Virginia Agricultural and Mechanical College (present-day Virginia Polytechnic Institute and State University) from 1872 to 1880 and, for the next two years, professor of mathematics at the Missouri School of Mines and Metallurgy. In 1883, he took a position as professor of civil engineering and commandant at the Agricultural and Mechanical College of Alabama, which subsequently became Alabama Polytechnic Institute and eventually Auburn University. He taught there until his death in 1907, having received an honorary LLD degree from Trinity College (present-day Duke University) and a PhD from the University of West Virginia in 1896. He was buried at Auburn.

As a Confederate general, Lane gave a courageous and competent performance, although apparently Robert E. Lee never had full confidence in him, passing him over twice for the rank of major general and division command. Lane's troops evidently regarded him favorably. They nicknamed him the "Little General" because of his modest height. When he was promoted to brigadier, the men of the Twenty-eighth Regiment presented him with a sword, a sash, and a saddle and bridle.

Collett Leventhorpe

1815–1889
Brigadier General of Home Guard

Collett Leventhorpe was born at Exmouth, Devonshire, England. His ancestors included members of the British aristocracy. He attended Winchester College until age fourteen and then had a private tutor. In 1832, at age seventeen, he received a commission in an infantry regiment in the British army. He served in Ireland, the West Indies, and Canada, obtaining the rank of captain of grenadiers. He resigned his commission in 1842, studied medicine for a time in England, and then sailed to Charleston, South Carolina, where he entered business.

On a trip to Asheville, North Carolina, he met Louisa Bryan, daughter of a prominent Rutherfordton family vacationing in the mountain resort town. Although Leventhorpe proposed marriage to Louisa, her father wanted him to improve his financial prospects before they wed. So he returned to Charleston to complete his medical education, graduating from Charleston Medical College with its highest honor. The couple was then married in 1849, and Leventhorpe presumably started a medical practice in Rutherfordton, where he became an American citizen. The 1850 census lists him as a physician, but other sources claim that he never practiced in that profession. If he did, though, it was not for long. His biographers wrote that the "casting off of his medical career seems merely to have been part of a pattern he would exhibit throughout his life: a constant searching, whether it be for profession, gold, valuable artworks, or lucrative inventions."

Following the outbreak of the Civil War, Leventhorpe took command of the Thirty-fourth Regiment North Carolina Troops in October 1861. Drawing on his experience in the British army, he effectively trained a well-disciplined and well-drilled regiment. In camp at Raleigh, he also had temporary charge of the Thirty-third and Thirty-seventh North Carolina.

In early 1862, his Thirty-fourth Regiment took up a position at Hamilton in Martin County to assist in protecting the Roanoke River and the Wilmington and Weldon Railroad from raids by Federal forces, which had occupied much of coastal North Carolina after an expedition by General Ambrose E. Burnside captured Roanoke Island in February and New Bern the following month. On April 2, he became colonel of the Eleventh Regiment North Carolina Troops and was assigned to Wilmington, where he commanded the district and its defenses until General Thomas L. Clingman relieved him in September. He and the Eleventh Regiment were then transferred to southeastern Virginia to protect the Blackwater River from possible Union assault.

Back in North Carolina in December 1862, Leventhorpe experienced his first combat at Whitehall (now Seven Springs) in Wayne County, on the Neuse River. There his regiment helped repulse a raid by Yankee troops led by General John G. Foster from the U.S. stronghold at New Bern. For their part in the action, Leventhorpe and his men received the praise of their commander, General Beverly H. Robertson. They continued to serve in eastern North Carolina as part of the defenses against U.S. attacks into the interior from the occupied coastal area. In early 1863, the Eleventh joined the brigade of General James Johnston Pettigrew, and in April it participated with that brigade—in the division of General D.H. Hill—in an unsuccessful attempt to recapture Washington, North Carolina, from the Federals.

Not long afterward, Pettigrew's brigade joined General Robert E. Lee's Army of Northern Virginia for its invasion of Pennsylvania. At the subsequent Battle of Gettysburg (July 1–3), Lee's army was soundly defeated by the Army of the Potomac, commanded by General George G. Meade. On the first day of fighting, Pettigrew's brigade charged the Union position on McPherson's Ridge. During the charge, Leventhorpe was wounded, having a bone in his left arm broken. As Lee's soldiers retreated into Virginia on July

4, Leventhorpe and other wounded Confederates were being transported in wagons when U.S. cavalrymen captured them. His captors placed him at the Theological Seminary at Mercersburg, Pennsylvania, where U.S. physicians cauterized his wound with nitric acid without the aid of anesthesia.

The Federals subsequently hospitalized Leventhorpe at the U.S. prison at Fort McHenry near Baltimore. His wound gradually improved but took a long time to heal. Union authorities transferred him in early 1864 to the prison at Point Lookout, Maryland. There, he and some of his fellow prisoners had the benefit of extra food and supplies made possible by money deposited in a New York bank for him by friends. After having been imprisoned for nine months, Leventhorpe was exchanged and returned to North Carolina for service. His effectiveness, however, was inhibited by his physical condition. In April 1864, he declared that his left arm and hand were "almost useless from the effects" of his Gettysburg wound. He also suffered a deterioration of vision, particularly in the left eye. The condition apparently resulted from an accident, and he had been treated for it for nearly three years. A surgeon concluded that service in the field would make the problem worse. Nevertheless, Leventhorpe continued to command troops in the Tar Heel State.

Governor Zebulon B. Vance commissioned him a brigadier general of the state's Home Guard, and he once again led soldiers in defense of the Roanoke River and the Wilmington and Weldon Railroad. He also commanded his Home Guard in a campaign against Confederate deserters and Unionists in Randolph County. He later would be accused of atrocities against their families, although his biographers maintain that he had no direct involvement in such acts of violence against civilians.

In February 1865, the Confederate War Department promoted Leventhorpe to brigadier general in the Confederate army and placed him under the command of General Braxton Bragg in North Carolina. On March 6, however, he declined the promotion, declaring that "I am under obligation to the governor of North Carolina to organize the state troops now assembled in Raleigh, and I am not able, consistently with this duty, to accept a command in the Confederate service with which I am honored." He might also have refused at least partially because of his resentment at having been denied promotion in the Confederate army for so long.

In any event, the state capital at Raleigh was indeed under threat of Union attack. The Federal army of General William T. Sherman was entering North Carolina from the south. Opposing him was the Confederate army of General Joseph E. Johnston. The two forces came to blows at the Battle of Bentonville in Johnston County on March 19–21, the last major battle of the war. After defeating Johnston at Bentonville, Sherman moved his columns to Goldsboro, where he joined forces with U.S. troops arriving from the coast and then pressed on toward Raleigh in pursuit of Johnston. As he withdrew northwestward, the Confederate commander abandoned the state capital to Sherman and moved toward Greensboro. In the meantime, Lee had surrendered to the Army of the Potomac and General Ulysses S. Grant at Appomattox Court House, Virginia. President Jefferson Davis and his cabinet took flight from Richmond to Greensboro and then to Charlotte and ultimate capture in Georgia. Leventhorpe was with Johnston's army when that general surrendered to Sherman at the Bennett Farmhouse in present-day Durham on April 26, 1865, ending the war for all practical purposes.

Leventhorpe returned to Rutherfordton for a short while, and then he and his wife moved to New York. He visited England for extended periods before returning to North Carolina and settling at Holly Lodge, near Lenoir in Caldwell County. He engaged in a number of business enterprises. In 1872, the Democratic Party nominated him for election as state auditor, but the Republican candidate defeated him. His health began to fail, and in 1878 he sold Holly Lodge and moved to Fountain, in the Yadkin Valley in Wilkes County. There he and his wife lived with her sister. He died in Fountain on December 1, 1889, and was buried at the Chapel of Rest Episcopal cemetery near Lenoir. He had no descendants.

Leventhorpe had a mixed experience as a general for the South and is often overlooked in Civil War history. He was once described as a "notably handsome man, nearly six and one-half feet tall in height, erect, and stately in bearing, and gentle as well as brave." His war wound and ill health might have retarded his achievements as a general officer and resulted in his relegation to command of the Home Guard. According to his recent biographers, J. Timothy Cole and Bradley R. Foley, as a "fortune seeker, an adventurer of sorts, and, indeed, a soldier, Leventhorpe seems never quite to have lived up to the promise that his abilities and life held. His truest calling was that of Confederate officer: respected by his men, brave in battle, yet marred by the promotion to Brigadier General that was so long delayed."

William Gaston Lewis

1835–1901
Brigadier General

William Gaston Lewis was born in Rocky Mount, North Carolina, on September 3, 1835. He attended the academy of Jefferson M. Lovejoy in Raleigh. Following his father's death, his family moved to Chapel Hill, where he enrolled in the University of North Carolina and graduated in 1855. He taught school for a time in Chapel Hill and Florida before joining the U.S. Survey Corps and working in Minnesota between 1857 and 1859. In the latter year, he returned to North Carolina as assistant construction engineer of the Tarboro branch of the Wilmington and Weldon Railroad.

Before North Carolina's secession and alliance with the Confederacy in May 1861, Lewis enlisted in the First Regiment North Carolina Volunteers. Soon promoted to third lieutenant, he took part with his regiment in the Battle of Big Bethel Church, Virginia, in June. He received promotion to first lieutenant and continued to serve in Virginia until the First North Carolina Volunteers' six months of service ended in November.

Lewis then joined the Thirty-third Regiment North Carolina Troops, where he was appointed major. He participated with that regiment in the defense of New Bern against the U.S. attack led by General Ambrose E.

Burnside in March 1862. Burnside's assault on New Bern followed his success at Roanoke Island in February. Winning a quick victory at New Bern, the Federals established their headquarters in the town and dominated much of coastal North Carolina for the rest of the war.

Although ultimately overwhelmed and forced to retreat along with the rest of the Confederate defenders, the Thirty-third Regiment put up a stiff defense, and Lewis demonstrated considerable courage, judgment, and leadership during the battle. He led several companies in repulsing assaults on a vulnerable point in the Confederate line. He also deployed his troops in two counterattacks. A fellow officer recalled that Lewis "had to fight to his front, right, and left, but still maintained his position…no one could have behaved with more coolness, bravery, and determination."

Because of his performance at New Bern, Lewis was appointed lieutenant colonel in the Forty-third Regiment North Carolina Troops. He fought with that regiment in the Seven Days Battles (June 25–July 1), in which the Army of Northern Virginia, commanded by General Robert E. Lee, halted the Army of the Potomac, commanded by General George B. McClellan, as it advanced toward Richmond. Lee's army forced the Federals to withdraw from the peninsula between the York and James Rivers. For the next few months, Lewis's regiment remained in the Richmond area, drilling and defending the Confederate capital.

The Forty-third returned to North Carolina in December to assist in repelling a Union raid on Goldsboro from New Bern. The regiment remained in the Kinston area and, in March 1863, took part in General D.H. Hill's unsuccessful attempt to recapture New Bern. It returned to Virginia in time to join Lee's army in its invasion of Pennsylvania. At the ensuing Battle of Gettysburg (July 1–3), the Army of Northern Virginia suffered a major defeat by the Army of the Potomac, then commanded by General George G. Meade.

During an attack on Culp's Hill on July 3, the colonel of the Forty-third, Thomas Kenan, was wounded and captured. Lewis then took command of the regiment and exhibited "bravery and coolness" in rallying his soldiers and leading their retreat into Virginia with the rest of Lee's army. Back on home ground, he and his troops served in various actions in Virginia before returning to duty in eastern North Carolina in the spring of 1864. There they helped thwart Federal raids from New Bern and then joined the force of General Robert F. Hoke in a successful attack to recapture Plymouth from the Union occupiers in April. Lewis was promoted to full colonel following that battle.

In early May, he was back in Virginia, where he took over command of the former brigade of Hoke, then under the departmental command of General Pierre G.T. Beauregard and charged with defending the southern approaches to Richmond. At the Battle of Drewry's Bluff on May 16, Beauregard's Confederates repulsed the Army of the James, commanded by General Benjamin F. Butler, and managed to bottle up Butler's army at Bermuda Hundred on a peninsula between the James and Appomattox Rivers, thereby preventing it from threatening Richmond. During the fighting, Lewis led his troops in an assault on Butler's right flank. About two weeks later, he received promotion to brigadier general.

Lewis and his brigade then joined the corps of General Jubal A. Early in the Shenandoah Valley. When Early's corps attacked Washington in an audacious raid in July, Lewis was seriously wounded, and he was absent from duty, recovering, until October. He then joined the Army of Northern Virginia in the trenches around Petersburg. By that time, the Federal army in Virginia, under the overall command of General in Chief Ulysses S. Grant, had forced Lee's army to take up those entrenched defensive positions south of Richmond. When Lee was finally forced to abandon his works on April 1 and flee toward Appomattox Court House, Lewis was commanding in the rear guard. On April 7, he was wounded in the thigh near Farmville and taken prisoner. He received parole soon after Lee surrendered to Grant at Appomattox Court House two days later.

Lewis returned to North Carolina and resumed his career as a civil engineer. He served as the state engineer for thirteen years, and for more than three decades, he applied his engineering knowledge and skill to the operations of a number of railroads. He also ran a hardware store in Tarboro and farmed for a time. He held the position of chief engineer for the North Carolina Phosphate and Swamp Land Surveys in 1885 and for the State Guard, 1885–1901. He was a member of the State Board of Education and chief engineer for swamplands, 1886–92.

Lewis died, apparently of pneumonia, in Goldsboro on January 8, 1901, and was buried at Willow Dale Cemetery in that town. He had married Martha Lucinda Pender of Edgecombe County in 1864. She was the cousin of another of North Carolina's Confederate generals, William Dorsey Pender. Lewis and his wife had seven children, one of whom died in infancy.

William MacRae

1834–1882
Brigadier General

William MacRae was born in Wilmington, North Carolina, on September 9, 1834, to a relatively wealthy family, and he had a private education. He quickly developed an interest in trains and railroads. When only sixteen years old, he left Wilmington and undertook an apprenticeship with J.P. Morris and Company of Philadelphia to learn the crafts of machinist and locomotive builder. At age twenty-one, he returned to Wilmington and began working in the machine shops of the Wilmington and Weldon Railroad. He subsequently became a locomotive engineer and track boss before studying civil engineering with his brother and father. He worked with them on projects in North Carolina, South Carolina, and Florida.

When the Civil War began, MacRae was working as a civil engineer for the Carolina Central Railroad at Monroe, in Union County. Before North Carolina's secession on May 20, 1861, and its quick alliance with the Confederate States of America, he enlisted in the Monroe Light Infantry as a private. On May 1, he was elected captain of that unit, which on June 11 was mustered into state service as Company B, Fifth Regiment North Carolina Volunteers. That regiment was ordered to the Yorktown area of

Virginia, where its designation changed to the Fifteenth Regiment North Carolina Troops. Its mission was to assist in defending eastern Virginia against Federal invasion from the coast. In early March 1862, it moved to Suffolk, where it joined the brigade of General Howell Cobb of Georgia.

In late March, Cobb's brigade was ordered to Goldsboro, North Carolina, to help defend against a possible Federal attack. A U.S. expedition led by General Ambrose E. Burnside had recently captured New Bern. The Union army established its headquarters in that town and continued to occupy much of coastal North Carolina for the rest of the war, threatening the state with raids into the interior. When the anticipated attack on Goldsboro did not materialize, the brigade was transferred back to Virginia and the peninsula between the York and James Rivers, where it fought in the Peninsula Campaign (March–July 1862). In that campaign, the Confederates, originally commanded by General Joseph E. Johnston, opposed the Army of the Potomac, led by General George B. McClellan, as it advanced up the peninsula toward the Confederate capital at Richmond. When Johnston was wounded at the Battle of Seven Pines on May 31, General Robert E. Lee relieved him and organized the Confederate force into the Army of Northern Virginia. Lee then launched an aggressive attack to drive McClellan from the peninsula in a series of engagements known as the Seven Days Battles (June 25–July 1). In the final battle at Malvern Hill on July 1, MacRae's troops sustained heavy casualties. Of the 692 soldiers present, the regiment lost 30 killed and 110 wounded.

After Malvern Hill, Cobb's brigade encamped in the Richmond area. At the Second Battle of Manassas (or Bull Run) on August 29–30, the Army of Northern Virginia triumphed over the U.S. Army of Virginia, commanded by General John Pope. During the battle, the brigade held a position at Gordonsville.

The next major action for MacRae came after Lee crossed the Potomac River and invaded Maryland in early September. Opposing the Confederate march was McClellan's Army of the Potomac. As the invasion unfolded, Cobb's brigade attempted to hold Crampton's Pass on Maryland Heights at Harpers Ferry, but it "was routed from the field." MacRae's regiment sustained losses of 11 killed, 48 wounded, and 124 captured. Nevertheless, the larger Confederate force, commanded by General Thomas J. (Stonewall) Jackson, took Harpers Ferry.

When Lee and McClellan came to all-out and bloody blows at the Battle of Sharpsburg (or Antietam) on September 17, Cobb's brigade arrived on the field as the fighting raged. Cobb was not present, having been placed on medical leave, and the colonel who replaced him became "very unwell" and withdrew. MacRae than assumed leadership of the brigade. He later reported its performance under his temporary command:

> *The brigade, numbering now about 250 men, moved eagerly and unfalteringly forward to within about 100 yards, then opened a destructive fire upon the enemy, largely outnumbering us. He made a short stand, and then fell back behind the hill. Three times did he try to advance, and was as often driven back by the galling fire of our gallant little band. We held them in check (momentarily expecting re-enforcements) until our ammunition was expended. Seeing no sign of support, I was constrained to give the command to fall back.*

In the battle, the Fifteenth North Carolina lost three killed, fifty-two wounded, and eight captured.

Having been repulsed by McClellan, Lee withdrew his army into Virginia. The Confederates remained in the Shenandoah Valley for a time and then moved to the Fredericksburg area. On November 26, the Fifteenth Regiment was transferred to the brigade of General John R. Cooke. At the Battle of Fredericksburg on December 13, Lee's troops dealt a devastating defeat to the Army of the Potomac, then led by Burnside. During the battle, MacRae's regiment leveled a withering fire on the Union troops as they attempted to assault Marye's Heights.

Following its victory at Fredericksburg, the Army of Northern Virginia went into winter quarters. Cooke's brigade was ordered to South Carolina and arrived there on February 22, where it was assigned to the coastal command of General Pierre G.T. Beauregard to help repel a Federal attack on Charleston. On the twenty-seventh, MacRae received promotion to full colonel. Although his brigade did not see combat in South Carolina, in May it was engaged in North Carolina in the Kinston area. MacRae's regiment lost two soldiers and had fourteen wounded in fighting at Gum Swamp. Cooke's brigade was then ordered back to Virginia, arriving at Richmond on June 7.

When the Army of Northern Virginia invaded Pennsylvania and suffered a major defeat at the famous Battle of Gettysburg (July 1-3), Cooke's brigade remained behind in the defenses around Richmond and repulsed an attack at the South Anna Bridge. After Lee's army had retreated into Virginia, it had to face an invasion by the Army of the Potomac, then commanded by General George G. Meade, the victor at

Gettysburg. Cooke's brigade clashed with the Federals at the Battle of Bristoe Station in mid-October. In an unsuccessful attack on Union lines, MacRae's Fifteenth Regiment lost fourteen men killed and eighty-seven wounded. Lee's and Meade's armies maneuvered and entrenched in the vicinity of the Rapidan River but did not engage in major action before going into winter quarters in December. MacRae and his regiment spent the winter of 1864–65 encamped with the rest of the brigade near Orange Court House.

In early May 1865, the Army of the Potomac was on the move. In overall command was General in Chief Ulysses S. Grant, whose objectives were to press Lee's army relentlessly, force it back toward Richmond, and secure its surrender. In the ensuing bloody Battles of the Wilderness (May 5–6), Spotsylvania Court House (May 7–19), and Cold Harbor (June 1–3), MacRae led his regiment. On June 23, he was promoted to the temporary rank of brigadier general and given command of the brigade of General William W. Kirkland, who had been wounded at Cold Harbor. He remained in charge of that brigade when, along with the rest of Lee's army, it entrenched at besieged Petersburg. In late August, his brigade took part in the Battle of Reams's Station on the Petersburg and Weldon rail line. The Confederates dislodged the Federals from their position and captured about two thousand prisoners. MacRae continued to command his brigade in a number of actions in defense of Lee's entrenched lines below Richmond. On November 5, 1864, he received permanent promotion to brigadier general.

MacRae was with Lee when, forced from his Petersburg defenses, he surrendered to Grant at Appomattox Court House on April 9. Afterward, MacRae returned to North Carolina and accepted appointment as general superintendent of the Wilmington and Manchester Railroad. He then relocated to Georgia, where in 1873 he became general superintendent of the Western and Atlantic Railroad. When his health declined, he resigned and moved to Florida, hoping a change in climate would improve his lung disease. His condition continued to worsen, however, and he started on a journey back to Wilmington to live out his last days. He died en route in Augusta, Georgia, on February 11, 1882. He was buried at Wilmington's Oakdale Cemetery.

MacRae rendered a capable performance as a regimental and brigade commander, receiving praise from his superiors, including Robert E. Lee. One officer said of him that "he could place his command in position quicker and infuse more of his fighting qualities in his men than any officer I ever saw…and gave the men an infinite faith in him and themselves which was never lost, not even when they grounded their arms at Appomattox." MacRae never married.

James Green Martin

1819–1878
State Adjutant General, Major General of Militia, and Brigadier General

James Green Martin was born at Elizabeth City, North Carolina, on February 14, 1819. He received his early education at an Episcopal school for boys in Raleigh. He entered the U.S. Military Academy at West Point in 1836 and graduated four years later, fourteenth in his class.

The U.S. Army commissioned him a second lieutenant of artillery and assigned him to duty on the coast of Maine. During the Mexican-American War (1846–48), he commanded a battery in the fighting at Monterrey and Vera Cruz. In 1847, he received promotion to first lieutenant and then captain. He fought in battles at Cerro Gordo, Contreras, and Churubusco. Grapeshot shattered his right arm at Churubusco, and it had to be amputated. For his leadership and bravery in the Mexican Campaign, he was given the brevet rank of major.

Following the war with Mexico, Martin served at Fort Monroe, Virginia, at a federal arsenal in Pennsylvania, and on the frontier in Nebraska Territory. Those assignments were followed by duty as quartermaster for Colonel (future Confederate general) Albert Sidney Johnston's expedition against the Mormons in Utah. Martin's last station in the U.S. Army was at Fort Riley, Kansas.

After North Carolina seceded from the Union and joined the Confederacy in late May 1861, Martin resigned his U.S. commission and returned to the Tar Heel State, where he joined a cavalry regiment with the rank of captain. In September, Governor Henry Toole Clark appointed him adjutant general for North Carolina, with the rank of major general of Militia. In that capacity, Martin held the responsibility for organizing and equipping North Carolina regiments for Confederate service. He demonstrated considerable initiative and skill in carrying out that task successfully. Through purchasing agents and a conscientious utilization of blockade-runners, he secured clothing, arms, and other war supplies for Tar Heel soldiers, who remained relatively well equipped and fed, at least for the first year of the war. He had, however, less success—at least partially because of a lack of support from the Confederate War Department—in his task of establishing and maintaining the coastal defenses of the state.

After about eight months as adjutant general, Martin petitioned for a command in the Confederate army. The War Department appointed him a brigadier general on May 15, 1862. A month later, he took command of the District of North Carolina, with a headquarters at Kinston. His mission was to assist in the defense of eastern North Carolina against Federal attack from the coast, much of which had been occupied by U.S. forces following the capture of New Bern in March by an expedition led by General Ambrose E. Burnside. The Union army made its headquarters at that port town and raided into eastern North Carolina for the rest of the war.

During the Seven Days Battles (June 25–July 1), on the Virginia peninsula between the York and James Rivers, General Robert E. Lee summoned Martin and a brigade of North Carolina troops to help repel the advance on Richmond by General George B. McClellan and the Army of the Potomac. Martin's brigade did not reach the peninsula in time to participate in the battles, however, and it returned to North Carolina.

Martin resumed duties as adjutant general for a short time, although he simultaneously retained his commission as a Confederate brigadier. Then, for some reason not entirely clear, he resigned that commission on July 25, but about two weeks later, he was reappointed and once again placed in charge of the District of North Carolina. In the autumn of 1863, he received new orders to form a brigade of four North Carolina regiments and encamp in the Wilmington area. In February 1864, he moved his troops northward to attack Morehead City and Fort Macon in support of General George Pickett's attempt to recapture New Bern from the Federals. Before going into major action, however, Martin learned that Pickett's assault had failed, and he and his troops returned to Wilmington.

When the Army of the Potomac, led by General in Chief Ulysses S. Grant and with General George G. Meade in tactical command, launched Grant's Overland Campaign (May–June 1864) to press Lee's Army of Northern Virginia back toward Richmond and force its ultimate surrender, Martin's brigade moved to Virginia to help defend the Confederate capital. After the gruesome battles at the Wilderness, Spotsylvania Court House, and Cold Harbor (May 5–June 3), the Army of the Potomac drove Lee's army into trenches around Petersburg. During that campaign, Martin and his soldiers, under the departmental command of General Pierre G.T. Beauregard, fought in the Battle of Drewry's Bluff on May 16. In that action, the Confederates thwarted the Army of the James, commanded by General Benjamin F. Butler, and succeeded in bottling it up at Bermuda Hundred, on a peninsula between the James and Appomattox Rivers, thereby preventing it from threatening Richmond. Four days later, Martin's brigade captured some of Butler's advance entrenchments at Ware Bottom (Howett's House).

While subsequently besieged in the Petersburg trenches, Martin requested to be relieved of field command. The stump of his amputated arm was causing him considerable pain, and his overall health had declined. He relinquished his command in June and returned to North Carolina, where he became commander of the District of Western North Carolina, presumably a less stressful situation. From his headquarters at Morganton, he had to deal with local conflicts between Unionist and Confederate sympathizers, organize local troops and defenses, and oppose Federal raids from eastern Tennessee. His final effort in the last days of the war was to resist the invasion of western North Carolina by the cavalry of General George Stoneman.

After the war, Martin studied law and launched a successful practice in Asheville, where he lived until his death on October 4, 1878. He was buried at Riverside Cemetery. While in New England in the 1840s, he had married Marian Murray Read, the great-granddaughter of George Read, a signer of the Declaration of Independence. She died, leaving him with four children, and in 1858 he married Hetty King, daughter of Charles King, the president of Columbia College.

Martin gave a credible, if not exemplary, performance as a field general. Robert E. Lee commended him for his service, and his troops apparently respected and admired him. They referred to him affectionately as "Old One Wing," in reference to his missing arm. But Martin's greatest contribution to the war effort was probably as state adjutant general, organizing and supplying North Carolina troops for the Confederacy.

John Wesley McElroy

1808–1886
Brigadier General of Home Guard

John Wesley McElroy was born in
Yancey County, North Carolina, on
April 7, 1808. Locally educated, he
became a prominent merchant, farmer,
and slaveholder in Burnsville, the county
seat. His financial ventures included the
production of ginseng. He served as Yancey
County's clerk of superior court from 1834
to 1846 and was on the board of trustees
for the local academy. Sometime before
1834, he was elected colonel of the county's
Militia regiment.

During the Civil War, he initially led his
Militia regiment in operations in the mountain region. Then in July 1863,
the state Militia was replaced by the Home Guard, which was made up
of men exempt from conscription (the draft) into Confederate service. At
that point, Governor Zebulon B. Vance promoted him to brigadier general,
with command of the First Brigade of the Home Guard in western North
Carolina. McElroy's daughter, Harriet, was married to Vance's brother,
Robert B. Vance, another of the Tar Heel State's Confederate generals.

As first colonel of the Militia and then general of the Home Guard,
McElroy had the difficult—probably insurmountable—task of trying to
maintain civil order and enforce state and Confederate war policies in

western North Carolina. Conflict in that region between local Unionists and pro-Confederates frequently resulted in bitter violence that included robbery, torture, and murder. The situation was made worse by Unionists who infiltrated the North Carolina mountains from eastern Tennessee, where they constituted a significant part of the population. U.S. troops also raided in western North Carolina from Tennessee. In the mountains, a guerrilla war raged between supporters of the North and supporters of the South. Militant Unionists—sometimes called bushwhackers, tories, or Yankees—raided Confederate troops and supplies and brutalized pro-Confederate families. Confederate troops and sympathizers—sometimes called destructives or secessionists— committed similar violence against Unionists.

At the core of this inner civil war lay the large-scale desertion among Tar Heel troops. Western North Carolina probably had the largest number of Confederate deserters in the state. They often banded together to prey on and terrorize local residents. Allied with the deserters were a number of draft dodgers defying Confederate conscription laws. "I am sorry to say," McElroy reported, "that our mountains are full of Deserters and Tories and I fear their numbers will be augmented by the last enrollment of Conscripts. I am confident that many will go to the mountains before they will go to the war and I fear they will do…much mischief…to our helpless inhabitants."

As time went on, McElroy found his mission more and more difficult. His brigade was undermanned, and he had trouble getting members of the Home Guard to turn out for service. He described to Governor Zebulon B. Vance the ever-deteriorating and chaotic situation in the mountains:

> *It has got to be impossible to get any man out there* [to perform Home Guard duty] *unless he is dragged out, with but few exceptions.…In fact, it seems to me, that there is a determination of the people in the country generally to do no more service to the cause. Swarms of men liable to conscription are gone to the tories or to the Yankees…while many others are fleeing east of the Blue Ridge for refuge…if something is not done immediately for this country, we will all be ruined.*

Suffering from a shortage of men and supplies on all fronts, neither the state nor the Confederate government could do much to assist McElroy. In the end, his tour as a general of the Home Guard in western North Carolina proved to be a thankless job that largely failed.

John Wesley McElroy

When the war ended, McElroy resumed his life as a merchant in Burnsville. He had been married to the former Catherine Poteat, but she had died in 1855. McElroy died in Robbinsville, in Graham County, on February 8, 1886, and was buried at the Old Mother Baptist Church cemetery in that town. His daughter, Harriet, had preceded him in death in the previous year.

William Dorsey Pender

1834–1863
Major General

William Dorsey Pender was born on
February 6, 1834, in Edgecombe
County. The son of a wealthy planter
and slaveholder, he was educated in local
common schools and, at age fifteen, clerked
in the store of his older brother, Robert. He
entered the U.S. Military Academy at age
sixteen, graduating in 1854, nineteenth in
a class of forty-six.

The newly commissioned second
lieutenant served first with the Second
Artillery Regiment at Fort Myers, Florida.
In 1855, he was transferred to the First
Regiment of Dragoons and engaged in
fighting Indians on the western frontier. He received promotion to first
lieutenant in 1858 and took post at Fort Vancouver in Washington Territory
the following year. He then was appointed adjutant of the First Dragoons,
with headquarters at San Francisco. In the winter of 1861, he returned east
for recruiting duty at Carlisle, Pennsylvania.

After the secession of South Carolina and six other states and the
formation of the provisional Confederate States of America, Pender
apparently thought that North Carolina would soon secede and join the
new Confederacy and that war was likely. Consequently, he resigned his U.S.

Army commission on March 9, 1861. All indications are that he believed in the right of secession and in the establishment of a Confederate nation. He portrayed the Federal government's efforts to maintain the Union as mere "revenge and stubbornness." He might have felt some moral pains about the cruel treatment of slaves by some owners, but he and his family owned slaves, and there is no incidence of his ever freeing any of them or advocating the abolition of slavery.

In the same month that he left the U.S. Army, Pender traveled to the first Confederate capital in Montgomery, Alabama, and applied for a commission in the artillery of the Confederate army. The War Department awarded him a captaincy and ordered him to Baltimore, where he was to recruit Southern sympathizers in Maryland and dispatch them south for enlistment. He left Baltimore about the time that Confederate artillery at Charleston fired on Fort Sumter. In response to that attack, President Abraham Lincoln called on loyal states for troops to suppress the growing rebellion. North Carolina refused that request but remained in the Union.

When Pender arrived back in his native state, Governor John W. Ellis commissioned him a lieutenant colonel and assigned him command of Camp Ellis at Raleigh. There, Pender set about drilling recruits of Colonel (later General) D.H. Hill's First Regiment North Carolina Volunteers. On May 20, North Carolina seceded from the Union, and it joined the new Confederates States of America the following day. About that time, Pender was promoted to colonel and given command of the Third Regiment North Carolina Volunteers, which became the Thirteenth Regiment North Carolina Troops. That regiment soon went into camp at Suffolk, Virginia. In August, Governor Henry Toole Clark, who had replaced the deceased Ellis, gave Pender command of the Sixth Regiment North Carolina State Troops. The Sixth's colonel, Charles F. Fisher, had been killed at the First Battle of Manassas (or Bull Run). The officers of the Sixth had petitioned the governor to appoint Pender commander of their regiment, and he set about improving morale, discipline, and equipment, which were all at a low level. Since his first command, Pender had established a reputation as an effective drillmaster and disciplinarian who looked to the welfare of his soldiers.

During the winter of 1861–62, the Sixth remained in quarters at Camp Fisher, several miles from the Potomac River. In early March, it marched to Fredericksburg, where it encamped until it was withdrawn to Yorktown. There it became part of the Peninsula Campaign (March–July 1862), in which the Confederate army, initially under the leadership of General Joseph E. Johnston, opposed the Army of the Potomac, commanded by

General George B. McClellan, as it advanced toward the Confederate capital at Richmond from the coast via the peninsula between the York and James Rivers.

As Johnston's force retreated up the peninsula from Yorktown, the Sixth Regiment participated in the skirmishing. The first major battle fought by Pender and his men came at Seven Pines (May 31–June 1), where Johnston ordered an assault on the Federals. Pender's regiment attacked from the left side of the Confederate line and nearly became cut off. Pender's calm leadership and an aggressive bayonet charge by his soldiers allowed the regiment to fall back and re-form to the right of Mississippi regiments.

On June 3, Pender received a promotion to brigadier general and was given command of the brigade of General James Johnston Pettigrew, who had been captured at Seven Pines. That brigade was in the Light Division of General A.P. Hill. General Johnston had been wounded at Seven Pines, and command of the Confederate force opposing McClellan fell to General Robert E. Lee, who reorganized it into the Army of Northern Virginia. Lee then launched a series of assaults known as the Seven Days Battles (June 25–July 1) to drive the Army of the Potomac from the peninsula.

During that campaign, Pender led his troops into action at Beaver Dam Creek, where they were repulsed by heavy musket and canister fire. At the Battle of Gaines Mill on June 27, Pender's regiments broke through the Union lines but had to retreat when they found themselves flanked. A second charge gained no advantage. In the subsequent fighting at Frayser's Farm, Pender's men captured a battery of rifled cannons and forced another to retreat before darkness fell and a shortage of ammunition forced them to halt.

The Federals retired to Malvern Hill, and on July 1 Lee ordered an attack on their heavily fortified position. The Confederate assault proved costly and failed to dislodge the defenders. As the fighting raged, Hill's division, including Pender's brigade, was held in reserve. After Malvern Hill, McClellan withdrew his force to Harrison's Landing, where he subsequently evacuated it from the peninsula. Although Lee's army had forced the Union forces to retreat and saved the capital, it had suffered heavy casualties. Pender's brigade lost one-third of its soldiers, more than eight hundred killed or wounded. Pender himself suffered a flesh wound in his arm, but it quickly healed.

In late July, Hill's division joined General Thomas J. (Stonewall) Jackson's command in opposing the advance of the U.S. Army of Virginia, led by

General John Pope. During that campaign, Pender took his troops into battle at Cedar Mountain and at Second Manassas (or Bull Run) in late August. At Manassas, he led a successful attack and sustained a slight head wound. His brigade suffered 157 casualties in the battle.

Encouraged by his victory at Manassas, Lee marched the Army of Northern Virginia into Maryland in September. As part of Hill's division, Pender's brigade participated in Jackson's capture of Harpers Ferry. In the subsequent bloody Battle of Sharpsburg (or Antietam), where Lee again clashed with McClellan and the Army of the Potomac, Pender's troops were assigned to protect against counterattack and "escaped serious fighting." Repulsed by McClellan at Sharpsburg, the Confederates retreated into Virginia, with Pender's men serving as part of a rear guard.

Pender's next major action came at the Battle of Fredericksburg in December 1862, when Lee's army mauled the troops of General Ambrose E. Burnside, then commanding the Army of the Potomac, as they attempted an ill-conceived and fatal assault on formidable Confederate defenses. During the fighting, a bullet passed through Pender's arm but did not break the bone. He continued to control his line of troops as his arm hung loosely by his side and blood ran down onto his fingers. He left the field to have the wound dressed but quickly returned. His brigade sustained the loss of 169 men at Fredericksburg.

The Army of Northern Virginia went into winter quarters in the area and then arose to combat the Army of the Potomac, commanded by General Joseph Hooker, at the Battle of Chancellorsville (May 1–4, 1863). It was there that the famed Stonewall Jackson was mortally wounded accidentally by North Carolina troops. Apparently, he issued his last battlefield orders to Pender. The Tar Heel brigadier had expressed concern that a break in his division's line might result in retreat. Jackson replied, "You must hold your ground, General Pender. You must hold your ground." When A.P. Hill took charge of Jackson's corps, Pender temporarily commanded Hill's Light Division until command passed to General J.E.B. Stuart. At Chancellorsville, Pender again sustained a wound. While standing behind an entrenchment on May 4, he was struck in the right arm near the shoulder by a spent bullet that had just killed an officer standing in front of him. Although the wound at first seemed not to be serious, Pender later admitted that it was worse than he had originally thought, and he suffered considerable pain for several weeks.

The Battle of Chancellorsville was probably Lee's greatest battlefield triumph. But the famous general expressed some frustration at Pender for not pursuing Hooker's retreating force on May 6. "Why General Pender," an exasperated Lee declared, "that's the way you young men always do....You allow those people to get away. I tell you what to do but you don't do it! Go after them! Damage them all you can!" Although Chancellorsville was a Confederate victory, Pender's brigade sustained heavy casualties, and the Army of the Potomac lived to fight another day. Following the battle, Lee reorganized his army, giving permanent command of a corps to Hill and promoting Pender to major general and assigning him to lead Hill's old Light Division. In urging President Davis to approve Pender's promotion, Lee reported that the North Carolinian "is an excellent officer, attentive, industrious, & brave...conspicuous in every battle & I believe wounded in almost all of them."

Lee's next plan of action called for the Army of Northern Virginia to invade Pennsylvania. There it came to blows with the Army of the Potomac, then commanded by General George G. Meade, at the famed Battle of Gettysburg (July 1–3). On July 2, Pender's division attacked the Federal defenses on Seminary Ridge. Near sundown, a shell fragment struck the general in the thigh, and he was forced to seek medical attention and relinquish command of his division to his subordinate, Brigadier General James H. Lane. Confederate defeat followed on the third day, with Lee's disastrous assault on Cemetery Ridge. On July 4, the Army of Northern Virginia began its retreat into Virginia.

Although he attempted to mount a horse, Pender had to be transported in an ambulance. At Staunton, Virginia, about two weeks later, his leg began hemorrhaging, and he managed to stop the bleeding by applying a tourniquet. But a surgeon could not repair the severed artery and therefore amputated the leg. Pender lived for only a short time after the operation, dying on July 18.

His body was transported back to Edgecombe County and buried at the cemetery of Calvary Parish Church in Tarboro. His death devastated his wife, the former Fanny Shepperd, whom he had married in 1859. She secluded herself in her room for three days when she learned that he had died. She was pregnant at the time and gave birth to a son in the autumn. The couple already had two other boys. She never remarried but rather supported her family by operating a school and serving as postmistress at Tarboro. When she died in 1922, at the age of eighty-two, she was buried beside her husband.

Pender proved himself a capable and brave commander who had the confidence of his superiors. At one point, as the war turned against the

Confederacy, Lee is reported to have exclaimed: "I am gradually losing my best men, Jackson, Pender, [John B.] Hood." But Pender's personal bravery and aggressiveness might have been a factor in the high number of casualties among his soldiers. That aggressiveness, and a strong sense of mission, sprang in part from a newfound religious zeal.

Early in the war, Pender underwent a religious conversion, which led to his baptism into the Episcopal Church in October 1861. His new enthusiasm for Christian dogma fueled his disgust at what he regarded as the evil Federal army and Northerners in general, whom he disparagingly referred to as "drunken rabble" and "unprincipled villains." Armed with the self-righteousness of his religious revelation, Pender came to view the Confederate war effort as a holy crusade sanctioned by God. His belief that he was on a divine mission perhaps led to what might be viewed as a reckless abandon in committing himself and his soldiers to battle. "My desire is to do everything that may gain favor with Christ and insure my salvation," he wrote to his wife on one occasion. His epitaph reads: "Patriot by nature, soldier by profession, Christian by faith."

James Johnston Pettigrew

1828–1863
Brigadier General

James Johnston Pettigrew was born at Bonarva Plantation in Tyrrell County on July 4, 1828. He received his early education at Bingham's Academy near Hillsborough and then attended the University of North Carolina at Chapel Hill. He entered the university at age fourteen and graduated in 1847 as valedictorian of his class.

Because of his skill in mathematics and his acquaintance with President James K. Polk and Secretary of the Navy John Y. Mason, both graduates of the University of North Carolina, he received an appointment as professor at the National Observatory in Washington, D.C., headed by the oceanographer Matthew F. Maury. Pettigrew, however, soon left that position to study law and travel in western Europe. James C. Johnston of North Carolina's Hayes Plantation—a friend of Pettigrew's father, Ebenezer Pettigrew, and the son's namesake—funded his studies and travel by means of a gift of $50,000. Returning to the United States, Pettigrew lived mainly in Charleston, South Carolina, from 1852 to 1861, where he practiced law as a junior partner in the firm of his relative James Louis Petigru. In

1856, he was elected to the South Carolina legislature, where he opposed reopening the international slave trade.

Pettigrew did not embrace secession with any enthusiasm. But he did believe that the nation was moving toward civil war over the issue of slavery, and he joined the South Carolina Militia. In 1859, he left the state to fight for Italy against Austria. During that conflict, he studied tactics and logistics, and upon returning to South Carolina, he began instructing its Militia companies. This second trip to Europe also led to the publication of a book about the history of Spain. Appearing in 1861 on the eve of the war, the work described traveling in that country and reflected Pettigrew's admiration for the customs and manners of the Spanish.

After Abraham Lincoln's election to the presidency in November 1861, South Carolina carried out its threat to secede from the Union. It was soon followed by six other slaveholding states, and they formed the provisional Confederate States of America, with a capital originally in Montgomery, Alabama. In April 1861, South Carolina troops led by Confederate general Pierre G.T. Beauregard fired on the U.S. garrison at Fort Sumter in Charleston Harbor, and the fort soon surrendered. Lincoln then called on the loyal states for troops to suppress the rebellion, and the Civil War began as four other Southern states, including North Carolina, joined the Confederacy.

During the events leading up to Sumter, Pettigrew served as chief military aide to South Carolina governor Francis W. Pickens. Following the surrender of the fort, he joined as a private the Hampton Legion, stationed in Virginia and led by General Wade Hampton of South Carolina. Soon, however, he accepted election as colonel of the Twenty-second Regiment North Carolina Troops (originally designated the Twelfth Regiment North Carolina Volunteers), which was deployed along the lower Potomac River from September 1861 to March 1862. Although offered promotion to brigadier general on several occasions and even interviewed for the position by President Jefferson Davis, he initially declined, arguing that every general should have led troops in battle before being awarded the rank.

Finally, however, he accepted a commission as brigadier to command troops in the Peninsula Campaign (March–July 1862). In that campaign, a Confederate force, originally commanded by General Joseph E. Johnston, opposed an advance on the new Confederate capital at Richmond, Virginia, by the U.S. Army of the Potomac, led by General George B. McClellan. The Federal expedition was launched from a coastal landing and progressed up the peninsula between the York and James Rivers.

While leading an attack at the Battle of Seven Pines on May 31, Pettigrew was wounded. A rifle ball penetrated the lower part of his throat, struck the bones of his shoulder, and cut an artery. Had not a fellow officer stemmed the flow of blood, he would have bled to death. He suffered further wounds during a Union counterattack, when he was shot again in the arm and bayoneted in the leg as he lay on the battlefield. When he regained consciousness, he decided that his wounds were mortal and refused to be evacuated, lying on the ground throughout the night. Federal soldiers took him prisoner and moved him to a hospital in their rear. They subsequently transported him to prison at Fort Monroe, Virginia, then to Baltimore, and finally to Fort Delaware. On August 5, he was exchanged at Aiken Landing, Virginia.

Returning to duty, Pettigrew received command of a brigade composed of the Eleventh, Twenty-sixth, Forty-fourth, Forty-seventh, and Fifty-second Regiments North Carolina Troops. In December 1862, the brigade transferred from Virginia to North Carolina to defend against Federal attack from the coastal region, much of which had been held by Union forces headquartered at New Bern since March. Pettigrew's troops helped thwart a U.S. raid toward Goldsboro and then participated in General D.H. Hill's failed attempt to recapture New Bern and his abandoned siege of Washington in March and April 1863.

The North Carolinian's brigade was back in Virginia in time to join General Robert E. Lee's Army of Northern Virginia in its invasion of Pennsylvania in late June. At the ensuing Battle of Gettysburg (July 1–3), Pettigrew's soldiers forced the retreat of U.S. troops from their position on McPherson's Ridge on July 1. When their division commander, General Henry Heth, was wounded, Pettigrew took over leadership of the division, including his and three other brigades. During the famed Pickett's Charge against Federal positions on Cemetery Ridge on the third day of battle, Pettigrew's troops were part of the failed attack that proved so devastating for Lee's army. In the assault over open ground, Pettigrew's horse was killed, and the bones of his right hand were shattered by grapeshot. But he had the hand placed in splints and remained on the field until the decimated Confederates withdrew.

As the Army of Northern Virginia retreated across the Potomac and into Virginia, Pettigrew commanded a rearguard defense. When attacked by U.S. cavalry at Fallen Waters, Maryland, on July 14, Pettigrew, because of his wounds, had difficulty controlling his frightened horse, which fell, taking the general with it. When Pettigrew regained his feet, a pistol round hit him in the left side and exited his back. Medical officers wanted to leave him in a nearby barn to recover, but he refused to risk capture again. He was then transported by litter across the Potomac and twenty-two miles to a house near Bunker Hill, Virginia. He died there on July 17, "probably from peritonitis." He was first buried at Raleigh and then reinterred at the family cemetery at Bonarva after the war.

Pettigrew was the most intellectual and cultured of North Carolina's generals, and he best epitomized the idealized and romanticized image of the chivalrous Confederate officer. In addition to having a keen grasp of mathematics, he was an accomplished musician and was proficient in four European languages. He also taught himself Hebrew and Arabic. He particularly admired the civilizations of the Spanish and Italians and intended to write a history of the Spanish Moors.

During his prewar days in Europe, Pettigrew served for a time as secretary of the U.S. Legation in Madrid, resigning when the wife of a candidate for that position asked him to defer to her husband. His humanitarianism and public service included poor relief and even nursing some victims of epidemics. His own health had been poor in childhood, and he continued for the rest of his life to suffer from sickness, including ague, yellow fever, eye infection, and breakbone fever. As his actions testify, Pettigrew's heroism on the battlefield was without question. Douglas Southall Freeman said about him that for "none who fought so bravely in the Army of Northern Virginia was there more praise while living or more laments when dead." His biographer, Clyde Wilson, appropriately labeled him a "Carolina Cavalier." Although considered a most eligible bachelor of gentlemanly temperament, Pettigrew never married.

Leonidas Polk

1806–1864
Lieutenant General

Leonidas Polk was born in Raleigh on April 10, 1806. His father was a prominent Revolutionary War veteran, banker, and politician. His mother was the former Sarah Hawkins, sister of a governor of North Carolina, William Hawkins. Polk received a local education and then attended the University of North Carolina at Chapel Hill in 1821–23. He left that institution to enter the U.S. Military Academy at West Point. There he roomed with the future Confederate general Albert Sidney Johnston and became friends with Jefferson Davis, who would become president of the Confederacy.

In his last year at the academy, Polk became a converted and devout member of the Episcopal Church. Following graduation, he served only a short time in the army before resigning his commission to attend the Virginia Theological Seminary. He was ordained in 1830, the same year that he married Frances Ann Devereux of Raleigh. Polk became assistant rector at Monument Church in Richmond but soon resigned because of ill health, which would plague him for much of his life.

In the summer of 1831, he left his wife and newborn son in Raleigh and began traveling in Europe in an attempt to regain his health. He returned to his family in October of the following year and occasionally preached in Raleigh's Christ Church. Encouraged by physicians to improve his physical condition through a "vigorous outdoor life," Polk left North Carolina with his family and settled on a large tract in Maury County, Tennessee, given to him by his father, who had speculated widely in Tennessee land. There he began operating a cotton plantation, on which he built a dwelling, Ashwood, and a hemp factory. He also accepted a position as minister of St. Peter's Church in Columbia, Tennessee, and divided his time between his plantation and his parochial duties.

In 1838, Episcopal authorities appointed Polk missionary bishop of the Southwest, a territory that included Arkansas, Texas, Mississippi, Alabama, Louisiana, and part of the Indian Territory. For three years, he traveled throughout that region, giving sermons, baptizing people, and consecrating churches. He then became bishop of Louisiana, where for the next twelve years he also ran a sugar plantation at Bayou la Fourche with hundreds of slaves. Because of large debts, however, he lost the plantation in 1854.

Polk was a strong advocate of southern rights and sectionalism and lent his support to the establishment of a university in the South for the education of southern Episcopal clergymen and laymen. Through his efforts and those of other Episcopal clergy and backers, land was purchased in Tennessee, and in October 1860, Polk presided at the laying of the cornerstone for the University of the South at Sewanee.

With the outbreak of the Civil War in the spring of 1861, President Davis commissioned Polk a major general in the Confederate army. The bishop laid aside his clerical duties and took up the mantle of war, claiming his summons to lead Southern troops to be "a call from Providence." Davis assigned him command of Department No. 2, which consisted of western Tennessee and eastern Arkansas, with headquarters at Memphis. Believing that the main threat to the Confederacy came from a U.S. thrust down the Mississippi River, Polk concentrated his efforts primarily on defending the river, to the neglect of other areas in his department.

Polk made another mistake when, in September, he dispatched troops—without consulting the War Department—to occupy Columbus, Kentucky, near the northern border of Tennessee. That maneuver gave the Confederacy no military advantage and actually led Kentucky—which, although a slaveholding border state, had attempted to remain neutral—to become allied primarily with the Federal government.

In early 1862, the Confederates were forced to evacuate Columbus, along with much of western Tennessee, as a Federal army commanded by General

Ulysses S. Grant moved up the Tennessee River after capturing Fort Henry on that river and Fort Donelson on the Cumberland River. Polk then found himself under the command of his old West Point roommate, General Albert Sidney Johnston, who at Corinth, Mississippi, reorganized the Confederate force into the Army of Mississippi. He divided his army into corps, giving Polk command of the First Corps, which he led at the Battle of Pittsburg Landing (or Shiloh) on April 6–7.

At Pittsburg Landing, Grant's army, supported by that of General Don Carlos Buell, ultimately defeated the Confederates after a hard-fought and costly clash in which Johnston was killed and replaced by his subordinate, General Pierre G.T. Beauregard. As the battle raged, Polk's troops charged and were driven back three times over the same ground. Beauregard led the Army of Mississippi to Corinth, where it withstood a siege and then evacuated to Tupelo. There, General Braxton Bragg replaced him. In the autumn of 1862, Bragg's army merged with the Army of Kentucky to form the Army of Tennessee, and Polk was promoted to lieutenant general and given permanent command of a corps.

At the Battle of Murfreesboro (or Stone's River), December 31–January 2, Bragg's force fought General William S. Rosecrans's Army of the Cumberland to a stalemate before retreating. Polk's corps incurred large losses and, despite repeated frontal assaults, met with scant success.

By that time, Polk had begun quarreling with Bragg, and he became leader of a group of officers seeking to have Bragg removed from command of the army. Polk dispatched letters to the War Department calling for Bragg's dismissal, and he and other officers even refused to obey the general's orders on a number of occasions. In response, Bragg tried to have Polk replaced. But the North Carolinian remained at the head of his corps until after the Battle of Chickamauga, Georgia (September 19–20, 1863), where the Army of Tennessee scored a victory against Rosecrans's force. The fighting had scarcely ended when Bragg dismissed Polk from command. President Davis, in an attempt to deal with the feud among the generals, transferred his friend Polk to take charge of the Department of Alabama, Mississippi, and East Louisiana.

Polk was deployed in that area until May 1864, when he and his troops moved to north Georgia to reinforce the Army of Tennessee, then under the leadership of General Joseph E. Johnston, defending against the advance of the U.S. Army of the Tennessee, led by General William T. Sherman. Polk's corps fought in the early battles of the Atlanta Campaign. In June, the Confederates had occupied a position just above Marietta, Georgia, about twenty-five miles north of Atlanta. At the top of Pine Mountain on the fourteenth of the month, Polk and a group of officers were observing the Union lines when they were spotted by Federal artillery, which began firing on them. Polk was killed instantly. According to Jack D. Welsh in *Medical Histories of Confederate Generals*, "A Parrott shell passed through his left arm, body, and right arm before emerging to explode against a tree. The trunk of the chestnut tree struck by the shell was still standing in 1902." Polk was originally buried in Augusta, Georgia, but his remains were reinterred in 1945 at Christ Church Cathedral in New Orleans.

Although he held the high rank of lieutenant general—at least partly through his friendship with Jefferson Davis—Polk had only limited success as a military commander. His seizure of Columbus, Kentucky, early in the war had been a tactical mistake with serious political consequences. His battlefield maneuvers brought high casualties and achieved little, and his quarreling with Bragg undermined the Confederate war effort. Polk and his wife had eight surviving children. A son was stillborn in 1833.

Lucius Eugene Polk

1833–1892
Brigadier General

Lucius Eugene Polk was born on July 10, 1833, in Salisbury, North Carolina. He was the nephew of General Leonidas Polk. At the age of two, he moved with his parents to Maury County, Tennessee, where they settled with other members of the Polk family. He graduated from the University of Virginia in 1852 and became a cotton planter in Phillips County, Arkansas.

With the outbreak of the war, Polk joined as a private the company known as the Yell Rifles in the Fifteenth Arkansas Infantry. The company was commanded by his friend, Captain Patrick R. Cleburne, who rose to command the regiment as colonel and then to the rank of major general in the Confederate army. Soon after joining the Arkansas regiment, Polk received a commission as lieutenant, and he and Cleburne served together until Polk's wounds forced his retirement from the army.

In northeastern Arkansas in the summer of 1861, Cleburne's regiment joined the force led by Brigadier General William J. Hardee. That force united with the army of General Albert Sidney Johnston at Bowling Green, Kentucky, where Hardee was promoted to major general and assigned a division. In February 1862, Johnston withdrew his army from Kentucky to Corinth, Mississippi, and reorganized it into the Army of Mississippi. Cleburne was promoted to brigadier general and assigned a brigade in Hardee's command.

As part of his friend's brigade, Polk and the Fifteenth Arkansas went into action at the Battle of Pittsburg Landing, or Shiloh, in Tennessee (April 6–7, 1862). In that hard-fought clash with many casualties, a Federal army led by General Ulysses S. Grant and supported by that of General Don Carlos Buell ultimately defeated the Confederates. Johnston himself was killed and succeeded by General Pierre G.T. Beauregard. Polk suffered a wound to the face but recovered quickly. Soon after the battle, he was promoted from lieutenant to colonel and given command of his regiment.

Following Pittsburg Landing, General Braxton Bragg, who had assumed command of the Confederacy's western army when Beauregard took a leave of absence, invaded Kentucky. During that expedition, Polk's regiment and Cleburne's provisional division, composed of his and another brigade, marched in the vanguard of General Edmund Kirby Smith's advance. They engaged and helped capture the Union brigades of Generals Mahlon D. Manson and Charles Cruft at the Battle of Richmond, Kentucky (August 29–30). Polk was wounded when a bullet grazed his head on the thirtieth, and observers remember him as "wild as a hare." While Polk was being moved to the rear for treatment, Cleburne stopped to talk to him and was also wounded.

Polk recovered in time to take the field on the day before the Battle of Perryville, Kentucky, on October 8. During the fighting, he suffered a third wound, this time to the foot. At Perryville, the Union army led by Buell overwhelmed Bragg's army and forced its retreat into Tennessee. Shortly thereafter, the Confederacy's Army of Tennessee was formed as the principal army in the west, under Bragg. On December 13, Polk received promotion to brigadier general and was given the old brigade of Cleburne, who had gone on to permanent division command. Polk led his brigade at the Battle of Murfreesboro, Tennessee (December 31–January 2). A final attack by Bragg on General William S. Rosecrans's Army of the Cumberland failed, and the Confederates withdrew to Chattanooga, where they continued to challenge Rosecrans's troops.

The two adversaries came to full conflict at the Battle of Chickamauga, Georgia (September 19–20, 1863). Assisted by reinforcements from Virginia commanded by General James Longstreet, Bragg's force drove the Federals from the field. Bragg then moved his troops to the heights around Chattanooga, facing Rosecrans. But there he hesitated and quarreled with his subordinates. In the meantime, the more aggressive Grant replaced the slow-moving Rosecrans, and on November 24 and 25, Grant's subordinate, General William T. Sherman, drove the Confederates off Lookout Mountain and Missionary Ridge. Despite the Confederate defeat, Polk received the praise of Cleburne and his other superior officers for his leadership in all three encounters. Bragg resigned his command in the west and left for Richmond, Virginia, to serve as an adviser to President Jefferson Davis.

Polk continued to lead his brigade effectively as the Army of Tennessee, commanded by General Joseph E. Johnston after Bragg's resignation, fell back through northern Georgia. His military career, however, soon came to an end in the Atlanta Campaign of the spring and summer of 1864, as Johnston's army attempted to halt the advance of the western Federal army, then led by Sherman. On June 16 at Mud Creek, Georgia, near Kennesaw Mountain, Polk received a devastating wound when his horse was shot from under him and a cannonball swept over his left leg, fracturing the bone. Surgeons removed the head of the fibula and the shattered parts, and stretcher-bearers transported Polk to Cleburne's headquarters. Although he recovered relatively well from the surgery and generally remained in good health, the injury left him incapacitated for service in the field. He returned on crutches to Maury County, Tennessee.

After the war, Polk resumed farming, although crippled by his wound. A Democrat, he served as a delegate to the party's national convention in 1884. Three years later, he entered the Tennessee Senate. He died on December 1, 1892, and was buried at St. John's Churchyard near Columbia, Tennessee. In August 1863, he had married his cousin Sallie Moore Polk, and they had five children.

One Confederate soldier, Sam R. Watkins, described Polk as having "long black hair that curled, a gentle and attractive black eye that seemed to sparkle with love rather than chivalry, and were it not for a young moustache and goatee that he usually wore, he would have passed for a beautiful girl. In his manner he was as simple and guileless as a child, and generous almost to a fault."

Gabriel James Rains

1803–1881
Brigadier General

G abriel James Rains was born in New Bern, North Carolina, on June 4, 1803. He received his early education at the New Bern Academy, graduating in 1820. He entered the U.S. Military Academy at West Point three years later, graduating thirteenth in a class of thirty-eight. Commissioned a second lieutenant, he undertook his first army assignment with the Seventh Infantry at Fort Gibson in the Indian Territory. He served in the Indian Territory for twelve years and assisted in the removal of the Choctaws from Mississippi. Apparently, he

also became friends with Lieutenant Jefferson Davis, future president of the Confederacy. He received promotion to first lieutenant in 1834 and to captain three years later. In 1839, he took command of Fort Micanopy and Fort King in northern Florida and oversaw their defense during the rest of the second war with the Seminole Indians (1835–42). During that conflict, Rains utilized the first of the explosive devices known as torpedoes or subterra shells (exploding mines) that would become his trademark during the Civil War. For his performance in the Seminole War, in which he was seriously wounded, Rains earned the brevet rank of major. He then had tours at posts in Louisiana and Texas.

Rains's next combat experience came when he participated in the Battles of Palo Alto and Resaca de la Palma during the Mexican-American War (1846–48). His service in that conflict concluded with his performing recruiting duty for General Zachary Taylor. After the war, he returned briefly to Florida. Acquiring the permanent rank of major and assignment to the Fourth Infantry Regiment, in 1853 he transferred to Washington Territory, where he led troops in campaigns against the Yakima Indians, before moving to Fort Humboldt in California. He was promoted to lieutenant colonel of the Fifth Infantry Regiment in June 1860. He was stationed in Vermont when word reached him in May 1861 that his native state had seceded from the Union.

Unlike some of North Carolina's Confederate generals who were serving in the U.S. Army when the Civil War broke out, Rains did not immediately rush to resign his commission and seek appointment in the army of the South. Not until the end of July 1861—after the First Battle of Manassas (or Bull Run)—did he resign his commission and offer his services to the Confederacy. He received a commission as colonel in the Confederate army and, in September, a promotion to brigadier general. He was originally assigned to command the First Division of the Department of the Peninsula. His unit came under the immediate command of General John B. Magruder and the overall command of General Joseph E. Johnston. Rains soon was transferred to command a brigade in the division of fellow Tar Heel General D.H. Hill. The Confederates were deployed on the Virginia peninsula between the York and James Rivers, east of the capital of Richmond. There, initially under Johnston's leadership, they fought in the Peninsula Campaign (March–July 1862) against the Army of the Potomac, commanded by General George B. McClellan, as it advanced from the coast toward Richmond.

Rains and his troops held a position at Yorktown. As McClellan began his siege, Rains's soldiers stood fast under heavy bombardment. He was cited for leading his men with "determination, devoted zeal, and gallantry." Seeking a defensive line closer to the Confederate capital, Johnston ordered a withdrawal up the peninsula. In the meantime, Rains had been experimenting with land mines, and as he evacuated Yorktown, his men planted those devices along the withdrawal route. Explosions killed a number of advancing Union soldiers, and McClellan and the Northern press denounced the use of such hidden weapons as uncivilized warfare. Some of Rains's superiors, most notably Johnston and General James Longstreet, also voiced their disapproval of his use of hidden mines. Longstreet ordered him not to deploy any more of them, but Rains defended their utilization, especially against night attack and to defend a weak position or withdrawal. Hill agreed with Rains. Ultimately, Secretary of War George W. Randolph ruled that the torpedoes, or subterra shells, could be used to defend works, halt a pursuit, or sink a ship, but not for the specific purpose of annihilating enemy troops.

Rains led his brigade into action at the Battle of Seven Pines on May 31, 1862. However, Hill criticized him for failing to assist during a frontal assault. Johnston was wounded in that battle and replaced by General Robert E. Lee, who organized the Confederate force into the Army of Northern Virginia and launched an aggressive campaign that forced McClellan to withdraw from the peninsula. During his attack, known as the Seven Days Battles (June 25–July 1), and its aftermath, Lee worried that the Federals might gain control of the James River and threaten Richmond. So he gave Rains a special assignment to oversee the mining of the river. For three months, Rains filled the James with "Sub-marine Torpedo Mortar Batteries," which were several artillery shells affixed with primers and mounted on an anchored wooden crib. Once in place, the shells sank just below the water surface, and they detonated when the hull of a vessel struck their primers. Rains also put barrel torpedoes in the water. These were common beer kegs made watertight and filled with powder.

With much of the mining completed, Rains relinquished the responsibility for "devising, placing, and superintending submarine batteries in the James River" to Lieutenant Hunter Davidson of the Confederate navy. The army general and navy lieutenant had cooperated in the mining of the river. Rains then took command of the District of the Cape Fear, which included the port of Wilmington and its protective Fort Fisher and other fortifications. His measures helped strengthen the defenses of the important blockade-running port in southeastern North Carolina.

His tour at Wilmington was short, however. He reported to Richmond in December 1862 to become superintendent of the Confederacy's Bureau of Conscription (the draft). Simultaneously, he began experimenting with explosive devices in the army's newly created Torpedo Bureau. Rains apparently did not let his duties as conscription officer interfere with his experiments in explosives, including innovations such as improved and more sensitive primers. He began to develop plans for mining Confederate ports with torpedoes. Hearing of his ideas, President Davis relieved him of his duties at the Bureau of Conscription and assigned him the task of preparing port and harbor defenses with explosives.

The president first dispatched him to Vicksburg, at the confluence of the Mississippi and Yazoo Rivers. Vicksburg held importance because if it fell to a Union siege by General Ulysses S. Grant, the Confederacy would lose control of the vital Mississippi River and become divided into two parts. The river port was commanded by General John C. Pemberton. But General Johnston was in overall command of the Confederacy's western forces, and because he had earlier deplored Rains's use of "deceptive warfare," Rains objected to being transferred to Vicksburg. Davis insisted, however, and Rains reached Jackson, Mississippi, in June 1863. There, he set up a laboratory for manufacturing explosive weapons. But Vicksburg fell to Grant's army on July 4, before Rains's efforts could prove effective. Nevertheless, his subterra shells did play a role in the Confederate retreat, at times scattering and killing elements of the pursuing Federal army.

Johnston then ordered Rains to the port of Mobile on the Alabama coast, where he remained for only a short time before Davis ordered him to Charleston, South Carolina. At that port city, Rains had the full support of the coastal commander, General Pierre G.T. Beauregard. There he mined the harbor with torpedoes and planted subterra shells outside the defensive line of Fort Wagner on Morris Island. As time went on, his concept of using mines increasingly gained acceptance among Confederate authorities. He began to promote the tactic of using his deceptive weapons extensively to defend Southern cities and even proposed it to state governors.

In February 1864, the War Department sent Rains back to Mobile, where he served under General Leonidas Polk, a fellow North Carolinian and classmate at West Point. He mined Mobile Bay heavily with torpedoes. One of them sank the U.S. ship *Tecumseh* in August, when the Federal fleet of Admiral David Farragut captured the port.

Rains was summoned to Richmond in May 1864 to help protect the Confederate capital from capture by the Army of the Potomac, then led by Grant in overall command and General George G. Meade in tactical command. By late June, the Federals had forced Lee's army into entrenchments at Petersburg, south of Richmond. Rains, in the meantime, had been given total control of "all duties of torpedoes" throughout the Confederacy and a free hand in installing water and land mines, for which he had been devising innovations and improvements. He heavily armed the James River, and in August, two of his subordinates managed to smuggle a time bomb onto a Union ammunition barge at City Point, Virginia. When it ignited, it set off explosions of thousands of rounds of artillery and small-arms ammunition. The barge and a large part of the wharf were demolished, 43 to 58 soldiers were killed, and between 40 and 126 were wounded. Property damage totaled $4 million. Even General Grant, who was holding an officers' meeting near the wharf, was showered with debris.

Rains continued to fortify the Richmond defenses. In October, he reported that he planted 660 torpedoes in the fortifications around the capital. The average number of shells planted daily grew to 100. As the war turned increasingly against the Confederacy, generals from Georgia through the Carolinas requested Rains's assistance, and he dispatched subordinates to help prepare defenses with explosive mines. Even Johnston, who had originally condemned Rains and his deceptive weapons, called for large numbers of them in the last days of the war, as he attempted to hold back the advance of General William T. Sherman into North Carolina.

Under relentless pressure by Grant and Meade, Lee finally had to abandon his entrenchments and flee westward, in hopes, perhaps, of connecting with Johnston. He surrendered to Grant at Appomattox Court House on April 9, 1865. Davis and his cabinet had already fled the capital, and Rains and his family accompanied them on the journey by train to Danville, Virginia. On April 26, Johnston surrendered to Sherman at the Bennett Farmhouse near Durham Station, North Carolina, effectively ending the Civil War.

After the war, Rains moved first to Atlanta and then to Augusta, Georgia, where he became a chemist for the Augusta Fertilizer Company. In 1874, he traveled through Raleigh, North Carolina, where he announced his plans to establish a fertilizer company at Charlotte. That venture never materialized, however, and three years later, he took a position as a clerk with the U.S. Army's Quartermaster Department in Charleston.

He continued his interest and experiments in deceptive explosive weapons, publishing articles on his ideas. He received a patent for an improved safety valve in 1873. In one publication, he defended the use of clandestine explosives in warfare, arguing that making war as terrible as possible would lead eventually to its abolition and to permanent peace. He declared that

> *could a piece of ordnance be made to sweep a battle field in a moment in time, there soon would be no battle field, or could a blast of wind loaded with a deadly mephitic malaria in one night [be] sent like the destroying angel in Sanacherib's army, or the earth be made to open in a thousand places with the fire of death...then and then only may we beat the sword into ploughshares, the spear into the pruning hook, and nations learn war no more.*

Rains moved from Charleston to Aiken, South Carolina, in 1880, in the hope of improving his health in a drier climate. He died in 1881 on August 6 (ironically, given his ideas about total war, the same month and day that the atomic bomb was dropped on Hiroshima in 1945). He was buried at the cemetery of St. Thaddeus Church in Aiken. In 1835, he had married Mary Jane McClellan, granddaughter of John Sevier, a North Carolina state senator, governor of Tennessee, and U.S. congressman. They had six children.

Stephen Dodson Ramseur

1837–1864
Major General

S tephen Dodson Ramseur was born
in Lincolnton, North Carolina, on
May 13, 1837. He attended schools in
that town and in Milton before enrolling
in Davidson College at age sixteen.
There he came under the influence of
Professor D.H. Hill, another of the Tar
Heel State's future Confederate generals.
Hill convinced him to apply to the U.S.
Military Academy at West Point and
persuaded Congressman Francis Burton
Craig of North Carolina's Seventh
District to appoint him.

Ramseur left for the academy in the spring of 1855 and received full
cadetship in January 1856. Although he generally disdained northerners
and preferred the company of his fellow southern cadets, he did befriend
George A. Custer, Wesley Merritt, and Henry A. du Pont, all of whom
served in the Union army during the Civil War. He graduated from the then
five-year program at West Point in June 1860, fourteen in a class of forty-
one members—the last class to graduate before the war.

His career in the U.S. Army was short. Commissioned a second lieutenant,
he served as an artillery officer at Fort Monroe, Virginia, and then briefly in
Washington, D.C. As war loomed, he resigned his commission on April 6,

1861, six weeks before North Carolina seceded from the Union. He received an appointment as captain in the Ellis Light Artillery in Raleigh. In the state capital in July, a thunderstorm caused his horse to panic and throw him to the ground, and the fall broke his collarbone. Then he came down with typhoid fever in September and recuperated at a private home in Smithfield.

Upon recovering, Ramseur reported to the division of General John B. Magruder at Yorktown, Virginia. Magruder's defenses were part of the Peninsula Campaign (March–July 1862). In that campaign, Confederate forces, originally commanded by General Joseph E. Johnston, opposed the Army of the Potomac, led by General George B. McClellan, as it advanced from the coast along the peninsula between the York and James Rivers toward the Confederate capital at Richmond. Ramseur quickly rose in rank, becoming colonel of the Forty-ninth Regiment North Carolina Troops in April.

When Johnston suffered a wound at the Battle of Seven Pines on May 31, General Robert E. Lee took command of the Confederate army opposing McClellan and reorganized it into the Army of Northern Virginia. Lee then launched a series of attacks known as the Seven Days Battles (June 25–July 1). During those engagements, Ramseur led his regiment with skill. At the final battle at Malvern Hill, a bullet broke his right arm above the elbow. He recuperated at a private residence in Richmond and received a sixty-day convalescent leave. After a month, he returned home to North Carolina, where he continued to endure considerable pain and paralysis in his arm. He went back to Richmond for further treatment in October.

The following month, Ramseur received a promotion to brigadier general and was given command of a brigade in Lee's Second Corps, led by the famed General Thomas J. (Stonewall) Jackson. But by mid-month, still suffering pain and paralysis, he returned to North Carolina. He was back in Richmond by early January 1863. His arm was in a sling, and it seemed as if it might prove permanently useless. Ramseur had, however, taught himself to write with his left hand and took command of his brigade once again by mid-January.

Lee followed his triumph at the Battle of Fredericksburg in December 1862 with another at the Battle of Chancellorsville in early May 1863. There, his Army of Northern Virginia overwhelmed the Army of the Potomac, then led by General Joseph Hooker, although Lee lost his valuable corps commander Stonewall Jackson, who was killed accidentally by North Carolina soldiers. General Richard S. Ewell succeeded Jackson in command of the Second Corps. Ramseur also was wounded when a shell fragment struck his leg, but he managed to remain on the field. After the action, he was hospitalized in Richmond and then convalesced in North

Carolina before rejoining his brigade in late May. His arm still troubled him and remained in a sling. On one occasion, a woman he was dining with had to cut his food for him.

Nevertheless, Ramseur was at the head of his brigade when Lee decided to invade Pennsylvania in late June. In the ensuing Battle of Gettysburg (July 1–3), the Army of the Potomac, then commanded by General George G. Meade, dealt Lee's army a devastating defeat. The final blow fell on July 3, when the Confederates' massive but disastrous charge up Cemetery Ridge proved fatal to their invasion of the North. On the first day of fighting, Ramseur's North Carolinians, who had already distinguished themselves at Chancellorsville, had helped drive Union troops from a heavily fortified position on Seminary Ridge. Following the disaster on Cemetery Ridge on the third day, however, Ramseur had to lead his brigade in the withdrawal, along with the rest of Lee's surviving army, back into Virginia and relative safety.

That safety was threatened in May 1864, when the Army of the Potomac, with the newly appointed general in chief of the U.S. Army, Ulysses S. Grant, in overall command and Meade in tactical command, began exerting unrelenting pressure on the Army of Northern Virginia in the area around Richmond. The first clash between the two armies came at the Battle of the Wilderness (May 5–6), where the Federals suffered heavy casualties, twice as many as their enemy. A large number of dead and wounded likewise followed at the Battle of Spotsylvania Court House, where Ramseur received another wound at the awful Bloody Angle on May 12. For the second time, a bullet struck his right arm, this one passing through below the elbow. Although he was out of action for a few days, he remained with his troops and on May 19 led them in an attack on the Federals' left flank. Near the end of the month, Ramseur's division commander, General Jubal A. Early, succeeded Ewell as commander of the Second Corps, and Ramseur assumed the leadership of Early's old division, contingent on his health's allowing him to stay in the field. Although still suffering from his wound and weak and exhausted, Ramseur remained at his post and on June 1 was promoted permanently to major general. At age twenty-seven, he was the youngest graduate of West Point to achieve that rank in Lee's army.

His promotion coincided with the Battle of Cold Harbor (June 1–3), in which Grant ordered a lethal and failed frontal assault on Lee's defenses that cost the Federals more than seven thousand killed or wounded. Despite that, however, Grant's so-called Overland Campaign managed to force the Army of Northern Virginia into entrenchments around Petersburg, south of Richmond.

On June 12, Lee ordered Early to transport his corps to the Shenandoah Valley to thwart the advance of the Federal force led by General David Hunter as it advanced up the valley to Lynchburg. If Hunter could capture the railroad hub in that town, he would deny the Confederates a vital invasion route and a source of provisions from the rich agricultural valley. Lee also ordered Early to drive north and threaten Washington and Baltimore in the hope of making Grant divert troops from the Siege of Petersburg. In a series of battles, Early chased Hunter from the valley; raided Maryland; burned Chambersburg, Pennsylvania; and threatened Washington in an audacious July raid. His campaign diverted two Union corps that could have faced Lee's soldiers at Petersburg.

Grant responded by ordering an aggressive commander, General Philip Sheridan, to organize the Army of the Shenandoah to drive Early out of the valley and deny Lee its resources. Sheridan's army set about attacking Early and destroying the crops and provisions that might fortify the Army of Northern Virginia. It defeated Early's troops in three battles: Third Winchester on September 19, Fisher's Hill on September 22, and Cedar Creek on October 19.

At Cedar Creek, Ramseur was mortally wounded. First he was slightly wounded, and two horses were shot from under him. As he mounted a third, a bullet struck him in the right side, passing through his lungs and lodging near the left chest wall. Before he could reach the rear— first on horseback, with an officer running alongside to keep him in the saddle, and then by ambulance—Federals captured him and took him to Sheridan's headquarters at Belle Grove. Both Union and Confederate surgeons attended him but considered his wound fatal. They administered laudanum, which produced unconsciousness. As Ramseur's life ebbed, his former West Point classmates George A. Custer and Wesley Merritt, U.S. cavalry generals, and Henry A. du Pont, a Union artillery commander, kept a bedside vigil. Ramseur died on October 20, 1864, and was buried at St. Luke's Church cemetery in Lincolnton. He had been one of Lee's most capable and aggressive generals. Douglas Southall Freeman characterized him as "among the most daring, hardest fighters in the Army."

The day before he received his mortal wound, Ramseur had learned of the birth of his only child, a daughter named Mary. He had married Ellen E. Richmond of Milton in October 1863.

Matt Whitaker Ransom

1826–1904
Brigadier General

Matt Whitaker Ransom was born on October 8, 1826, in Warren County, North Carolina. He attended Warrenton Academy and then the University of North Carolina at Chapel Hill, where he studied law in his last year, graduating in 1847. He was immediately admitted to the bar and began practicing law in Warrenton. His interest in politics led him first to join the Whig Party and then, when that party began to fade in the 1850s, to ally with the Democrats. In 1852, the state legislature elected him attorney general of North Carolina. In the following year, he married Martha Anne Exum of Northampton County and moved to Verona, her plantation on the Roanoke River. He served in the state House of Representatives from 1858 to 1861.

When Abraham Lincoln was elected president in November 1860, South Carolina quickly left the Union and was soon joined by six other states, which formed the provisional Confederate States of America, with its original capital at Montgomery, Alabama. The North Carolina General Assembly appointed Ransom one of three commissioners to go to Montgomery and observe the convention establishing the Confederate government and constitution. But North Carolina remained in the United States and did not secede until after Confederate artillery fired on Fort Sumter in the harbor of Charleston, South Carolina, in April 1861 and Lincoln called on the states for troops to suppress the rebellion. On May 20, the Tar Heel State's Secession Convention voted to secede, and the state quickly joined the Confederacy, along with three other slaveholding states—Virginia, Arkansas, and Tennessee—that had been holding out. As it was for a number of other political leaders in North Carolina, Lincoln's call for troops was the final determinant of political loyalty for Ransom. He abandoned any residual Unionism that he harbored and embraced secession.

He joined the First Regiment North Carolina State Troops and was quickly appointed lieutenant colonel and second in command. The regiment was ordered to the area around the Confederate capital at Richmond, Virginia, in July and then transferred back to eastern North Carolina in late March 1862. On April 21, Ransom was promoted to colonel of the Thirty-fifth Regiment North Carolina Troops, then encamped below Kinston, North Carolina. That regiment was part of the brigade commanded by his brother, General Robert Ransom Jr.

When Matt W. Ransom took charge of the Thirty-fifth, the powerful U.S. Army of the Potomac, led by General George B. McClellan, was advancing from the Virginia coast toward the Confederate capital at Richmond along the peninsula between the York and James Rivers. The Confederate force opposing him in the Peninsula Campaign (March–July 1862) was originally commanded by General Joseph E. Johnston. As part of his brother's brigade, Ransom's regiment transferred to Virginia to assist in repelling the Union attack, arriving at Petersburg on June 21. In the meantime, Johnston had been wounded at the Battle of Seven Pines on May 31 and was succeeded by General Robert E. Lee, who organized the troops defending Richmond into the Army of Northern Virginia. Lee then launched a series of aggressive attacks on the Federals known as the Seven Days Battles (June 25–July 1).

At the final engagement of that campaign, the Battle of Malvern Hill (July 1), Lee's troops attacked McClellan's heavily fortified position of massed artillery and infantry and sustained heavy casualties. Ransom's Thirty-fifth Regiment lost 18 soldiers killed, 91 wounded, and 18 missing. A bullet struck Ransom's right arm, rendering it temporarily useless, and a piece of shrapnel hit him in the right side. He was transported to the rear. Despite the high casualties on July 1, Lee's relentless offensive led to the evacuation of the Army of the Potomac from the peninsula.

Following Malvern Hill, the Thirty-fifth encamped and operated in the area of Petersburg and Richmond before joining the main body of the Army of Northern Virginia as it marched northward into Maryland. En route, Ransom and his troops participated in the capture of Harpers Ferry, before arriving on the field the day before the Battle of Sharpsburg (or Antietam) on September 17. In that bloody struggle—where Ransom's regiment had three men killed and twenty-three wounded—McClellan's Army of the Potomac forced the retreat of Lee's Confederates into Virginia. Ransom led his troops with his right arm still in a sling. He received a furlough in October to help him recover from his wound and returned to duty in December.

McClellan's failure to pursue and destroy Lee's army led President Abraham Lincoln to replace him with General Ambrose E. Burnside, who steered the Army of the Potomac into a disastrous defeat at the Battle of Fredericksburg in December. The Federals attacked the Confederates' heavily fortified position atop Marye's Heights and endured a virtual slaughter. Their casualties numbered 12,700 killed and wounded. The Thirty-fifth North Carolina had 9 men killed and 20 wounded.

In early January 1863, Ransom's regiment, along with the rest of his brother's brigade, moved to Kenansville, North Carolina, to guard the Wilmington and Weldon Railroad, a vital line for supplying Lee's troops in Virginia from the port of Wilmington. Since early 1862, the Union army had controlled much of coastal North Carolina and, from its headquarters at New Bern, threatened to sever the rail line. In February 1863, the Thirty-fifth was transferred with the brigade to the Wilmington area, then in late March to Goldsboro, and then to an outpost near Kinston in April. Ransom and his soldiers did not take part in General D.H. Hill's failed efforts to recapture the North Carolina towns of New Bern and Washington from the Federals in March and early April.

General Lee soon summoned them and the rest of their brigade back to Virginia to protect the Richmond area while the main force of his army marched to Pennsylvania. The Army of Northern Virginia began its invasion in late June, which culminated in a major defeat for the Confederates at the Battle of Gettysburg (July 1–3) by the Army of the Potomac, commanded by General George G. Meade. Following its ill-conceived and disastrous charge on Cemetery Ridge on the third day of fighting, the Army of Northern Virginia retreated across the Potomac River. Meanwhile, back in Virginia, Robert Ransom had been promoted to major general and given command of a division. Matt W. Ransom received a promotion to brigadier general and took over leadership of his brother's former brigade.

His newly assigned brigade took part in a number of skirmishes in the area of Richmond and Petersburg and then, in late July, transferred back to North Carolina to protect the Wilmington and Weldon Railroad. It went into winter quarters at Weldon in December, and its units performed outpost duty on the Roanoke River. In January 1864, the brigade departed from Weldon to assist in General George Pickett's aborted attempt to recapture New Bern.

Returning to headquarters at Weldon, Ransom's troops took part in a number of skirmishes in southeastern Virginia and northeastern North Carolina before participating in General Robert F. Hoke's recapture of the Roanoke River town of Plymouth in April. Hoke had to call off his subsequent attempt to seize New Bern, however, when Lee summoned his command to the Petersburg area. Ransom's brigade arrived there on May 10.

Lee needed all of the force he could muster to oppose the onslaught of the Army of the Potomac as it pressed the Army of Northern Virginia back toward Richmond. In overall command of the U.S. troops in the campaign was General in Chief Ulysses S. Grant, with General George G. Meade in tactical command. The Federals suffered heavy casualties in the subsequent Battles of the Wilderness (May 5–6), Spotsylvania Court House (May 7–19), and Cold Harbor (June 1–3), but they ultimately forced Lee's army into entrenchments at Petersburg. During that campaign, Ransom's brigade fought at the Battle of Drewry's Bluff (May 16) and then helped bottle up the troops of General Benjamin F. Butler at Bermuda Hundred before moving to Petersburg, where it was involved in heavy fighting on June 16 and 17. Ransom, though, had been wounded again, this time while rallying some of his men at Wooldridge's Hill on May 14. A bullet shattered both bones of his left forearm. Surgeons wanted to amputate, but he insisted on keeping the arm intact, so they removed the shattered bone and left the limb to heal. Ransom's left arm thus became shorter than his right, but the hand remained functional. He was evacuated to Richmond to recuperate but returned to duty on October 13.

Ransom's soldiers continued to serve in the Petersburg trenches. In the famed Battle of the Crater (July 30), in which U.S. troops temporarily broke through the Confederate works with a large land mine, the brigade lost fourteen men killed, sixty wounded, and eight missing. In August, it took part in attempts to drive the Federals away from the Petersburg and Weldon Railroad and in an attack on the Union position at Globe Tavern. Ransom's troops remained in the trenches until March 1865, when they participated in an assault on Fort Stedman. But there a massive Federal counterattack repelled the Confederates, and Ransom's brigade sustained a large number of casualties. The brigade next fought in actions near Hatcher's Run and Five Forks, on the right of the Confederate line. Again, the brigade suffered severe casualties. At Five Forks on April 1, Ransom, his left arm still in a sling, had two horses killed under him. With only one good arm, he had difficulty freeing himself and escaping injury from the dying second horse, which had collapsed and pinned him to the ground.

On April 2, the Army of the Potomac breached Lee's defenses, and his army began fleeing westward. During the flight, Ransom's brigade fought as part of a rear guard. Grant soon blocked Lee's retreat, and the Confederate general surrendered to him at Appomattox Court House on April 9. Ransom and the remnants of his brigade were present.

After the war, Ransom returned to North Carolina to farm and practice law. In 1872, he took a seat in the U.S. Senate that had been won by former governor Zebulon B. Vance but denied him because of political disqualifications. Ransom served in the Senate until 1895, when President Grover Cleveland appointed him minister to Mexico, a position he held for two years. He died in Northampton County on October 8, 1904, and was buried at Verona. He and Martha Anne had eight children.

Robert Ransom Jr.

1828–1892
Major General

R obert Ransom Jr. was born in Warren County, North Carolina, on February 12, 1828. He attended academies in Warren and Franklin Counties and then the U.S. Military Academy at West Point, graduating in 1850. He received his commission and a posting at Fort Leavenworth, Kansas, and then further frontier assignments in the Southwest, where he contracted cholera.

In 1854, Ransom served at West Point for a year as a cavalry instructor. He returned to Kansas as adjutant of the First Cavalry, where his duties included keeping the peace between warring factions that had invaded the territory since passage of the Kansas-Nebraska Act, which introduced the concept of popular sovereignty in settling the question of the extension of slavery into the West.

Throughout his military career, Ransom endured ill health. A broken arm and wrist in childhood left him with weakness in the left arm for the rest of his life. He had to take sick leave in the summer of 1856 after he developed fever and inflammation of the bowels. Another leave followed a bout of pneumonia in February 1857. In March 1858, he began hemorrhaging in the lungs and received an extended leave of absence. In August, he contracted typhoid fever. When his health improved in 1859, he led a unit of recruits to Fort Riley, Kansas, and then assumed duties at Fort Wise, Colorado. He received promotion to captain in January 1861.

Ransom's service in the U.S. Army, however, soon came to an end. After North Carolina seceded from the Union and allied with the Confederacy in May 1861, he joined the Ninth Regiment North Carolina State Troops (First Regiment North Carolina Cavalry), which organized at Camp Beauregard in Warren County on August 18. The governor appointed him colonel of the regiment, to rank from May 16. The regiment was ordered to Richmond, Virginia, on October 7, then to Manassas Junction, where it was assigned to the cavalry brigade of General J.E.B. Stuart. Ransom saw his first action in November, when he led twenty men from each of his companies on a scouting expedition and drove off a Federal detachment at Vienna, Virginia. The regiment performed picket and scouting duty on the line at Centerville for the rest of the winter.

In March 1862, Ransom and his soldiers received orders to move to Kinston, North Carolina, to help protect the eastern part of the state from further invasions by U.S. troops. A Federal expedition led by General Ambrose E. Burnside had captured New Bern on March 14 and then occupied much of the coastal region. On March 18, Ransom—with promotion to brigadier general, dating from March 1—took command of the former brigade of General Samuel French. That brigade included his brother Matt's Thirty-fifth Regiment North Carolina Troops. The Seventh Regiment North Carolina State Troops and the Twenty-fifth Regiment North Carolina Troops were added to Ransom's new brigade, and the cavalry and foot artillery were transferred out.

In Virginia, the U.S. Army of the Potomac, commanded by General George B. McClellan, had landed on the coast and begun a march toward the Confederate capital at Richmond. It moved along the peninsula between the York and James Rivers. General Joseph E. Johnston originally commanded the Confederate army opposing McClellan in the Peninsula Campaign (March–July 1862). Ransom's brigade responded to orders to reinforce Johnston and arrived in the Petersburg area on June 21. In the meantime, Johnston had been wounded at the Battle of Seven Pines on May 31. General Robert E. Lee took over his command, reorganized it into the Army of Northern Virginia, and launched a series of attacks against McClellan known as the Seven Days Battles (June 25–July 1). At the Battle of Malvern Hill, the final one of the campaign, Ransom's brigade attacked massed Federal infantry and artillery and was repulsed with heavy casualties. In fact, Lee's entire force lost a large number killed and wounded. Nevertheless, his seven-day offensive resulted in the Union army's evacuating the peninsula.

After Malvern Hill, the brigade deployed in the vicinity of Petersburg and Richmond before joining the main force of Lee's army for its invasion northward into Maryland. The brigade took part in the capture of Harpers Ferry, Virginia, before fighting in the Battle of Sharpsburg (or Antietam) on September 17. That battle produced some of the severest casualties of the war for both the Army of Northern Virginia and McClellan's Army of the Potomac. It resulted in Lee's withdrawing his troops into Virginia.

McClellan, however, failed to pursue and destroy the retreating Confederate army. So President Abraham Lincoln replaced him with Burnside, who led the Army of the Potomac into catastrophe at the Battle of Fredericksburg, Virginia, in December. There Union troops assaulted the heavily fortified Confederate position on Marye's Heights and sustained tremendous casualties, numbering 12,700 killed or wounded. Ransom paid tribute to their courage when he called them "as brave and determined foes as ever did battle." He also praised his own troops, noting that among the victorious Confederates, "none were more honorably distinguished than the sons of North Carolina."

In early January 1863, Ransom's brigade traveled to Kenansville, North Carolina, to defend the Wilmington and Weldon Railroad from destruction by Federal troops occupying the coast. The rail line was a vital route for supplying Lee's army in Virginia. After about a month, the brigade deployed in the vicinity of Wilmington, next at Goldsboro in March, and then at Kinston, where it helped drive Union raiders back to New Bern. While at Kinston, Ransom became ill again and took leave, but he was back on duty in May, in time to move his troops to the area around Petersburg and Richmond.

Lee had ordered them to Virginia to defend Richmond and Petersburg while his main army invaded Pennsylvania in late June. That invasion resulted in a devastating Confederate defeat at the Battle of Gettysburg (July 1–3) by the Army of the Potomac, then commanded by General George G. Meade. Lee's shocked and depleted army retreated into Virginia. In the meantime, Ransom had been promoted to major general and given command of a division and the responsibility for the defense of the Confederate capital. But in July, illness once again disabled him, and he had to take another leave. When he returned to duty, he was assigned command of the District of Southwestern Virginia and East Tennessee, where he commanded minor operations in the Knoxville Campaign (November–December 1863), in which the Confederate forces of General James Longstreet failed in an attack on the troops of Burnside, who had been transferred from the eastern theater.

By the spring of 1864, Ransom was back leading his division in the Richmond area, in time to assist in defending against General Ulysses S. Grant's Overland Campaign (May–June) to attack Lee's army with unrelenting pressure and force it back toward the Confederate capital. Grant had been appointed general in chief of the U.S. Army and had personally taken charge of the Army of the Potomac's overall operations against Lee, with Meade remaining in tactical command. The Federals suffered heavy losses in the ensuing Battles of the Wilderness (May 5–6), Spotsylvania Court House (May 7–19), and Cold Harbor (June 1–3), but they ultimately forced the Army of Northern Virginia into trenches at Petersburg. During the campaign, Ransom's soldiers fought under General Pierre G.T. Beauregard at the Battle of Drewry's Bluff (May 16) and helped bottle up the army of General Benjamin F. Butler at Bermuda Hundred.

Ransom left Petersburg in June to assume command of cavalry in the corps of General Jubal A. Early in the Shenandoah Valley. Lee ordered Early to halt the progress of the Federals led by General David Hunter as they advanced up the valley to Lynchburg. If Hunter captured the railroad junction in that town, he would deny the Confederates a vital invasion route and a source of provisions from the rich agricultural valley. Early chased Hunter from the valley; raided Maryland; burned Chambersburg, Pennsylvania; and threatened Washington in a daring raid. That raid became Ransom's last combat action in the war. He reported that he and his soldiers "came within 100 yards of the defensive works" of the U.S. capital.

Another episode of illness struck him, and he took yet another leave in July 1864. While recovering, he presided over a court of inquiry concerning alleged outrages committed by the troops of General John Morgan in Kentucky in September. Two months later, he commanded the defenses at Charleston, South Carolina, but he had to abandon that post just after Christmas because of illness. He was at home on sick leave when the war ended in April 1865.

After the war, Ransom worked as a freight agent and town marshal in Wilmington until 1867. He then sold railroad supplies until 1875, when he began farming near Richmond, Virginia, where he continued to endure bad health. In 1878, he took a position as assistant to the U.S. civil engineer at New Bern, attempting to improve rivers and harbors in North Carolina. He died in that town on January 14, 1892, and was buried there in Cedar Grove Cemetery beside his first wife, Mary Elizabeth Huntt Ransom, whom he had married in 1856. They had nine children, and she died in 1881. In 1884, he married a widow, Katherine DeWitt Willcox Lumpkin, and they had three more children.

William Paul Roberts

1841–1910
Brigadier General

William Paul Roberts was born in Gates County on July 11, 1841. He received limited formal education in local schools but was teaching in a small school in the county when the war began. He enlisted in Company C of the Nineteenth Regiment North Carolina Troops (Second Regiment North Carolina Cavalry) on June 10, 1861. He served as orderly sergeant but quickly rose to the rank of second lieutenant, with his promotion to date from September 30. In December, the regiment, assigned to the Department of the Pamlico, under General Lawrence O'Bryan Branch, encamped in the vicinity of the port town of New Bern.

A U.S. expedition led by General Ambrose E. Burnside captured New Bern on March 14, 1862. The Federals had already seized Roanoke Island and forts on the Outer Banks. With their headquarters established at New Bern, they would occupy much of coastal North Carolina for the rest of the war, controlling the sounds and raiding the interior along the rivers. Roberts's regiment was held in reserve during the Battle of New Bern and fled to Kinston with the rest of the Confederate defenders when Burnside's troops routed them and took the town.

At Kinston, the regiment was assigned to the brigade of General Robert Ransom Jr., under the overall command of Branch. For the next six months, detachments, including Roberts's Company C, performed picket and scouting duty in eastern North Carolina. In September, the regiment was ordered to Virginia, with Companies C and K remaining behind in the Tar Heel State. Two months later, the Nineteenth—without Companies C and K—officially became part of General Robert E. Lee's Army of Northern Virginia and was placed in the brigade of Lee's son, General William H.F. Lee, in the cavalry corps of General J.E.B. Stuart.

Roberts's company was still not with the regiment during the Battle of Fredericksburg on December 13, 1862. In that battle, the Army of the Potomac, commanded by Burnside, suffered a catastrophic defeat when it attacked the Army of Northern Virginia's heavily fortified position on Marye's Heights. Following the battle, the main body of the Nineteenth Regiment went into winter camp in Virginia. Company C, however, remained on picket duty along the Roanoke River in North Carolina.

At the Battle of Chancellorsville (May 1–5, 1863), Lee's army dealt the Army of the Potomac, then commanded by General Joseph Hooker, another devastating defeat. Before the battle, the Nineteenth, with Roberts still on special duty, picketed the fords along the Rappahannock River and conducted raids on the enemy. During the main fighting, it occupied a position on the left of Lee's army.

Meanwhile, Companies C and K had participated in an attack on the Federals in the town of Washington, North Carolina, on September 6, 1862. Soon after that, the two companies received orders to rejoin their regiment in Virginia. En route, they were sidetracked at Petersburg and ordered to report to General Junius Daniel at Drewry's Bluff, where they performed garrison and picket duty and arrested deserters. Further orders routed them to southeastern Virginia, where they came under the command of General James Longstreet and engaged in a number of skirmishes. They finally rejoined the Nineteenth Regiment and Stuart's corps at Brandy Station on May 20, 1863. By that time, Roberts had been promoted to first lieutenant, rank to date from May 1.

The Nineteenth then fought against Hooker's troops at the Battle of Brandy Station on June 9. That battle, a prelude to Lee's invasion of Pennsylvania, has been considered the "first true cavalry combat of the war," and the largest. In late June, the Army of Northern Virginia marched into Pennsylvania. In the ensuing Battle of Gettysburg (July 1–3), the Army of the Potomac, commanded at that time by General George G. Meade, inflicted a large defeat on Lee's army, which retreated into Virginia. During the invasion of Pennsylvania, Roberts's regiment rode in Stuart's controversial reconnaissance away from the main Confederate body. It took part in the battle on July 3 and then fought in rearguard actions as the Army of Northern Virginia withdrew across the Potomac River. In August, Roberts was promoted to captain.

Back in Virginia, the Nineteenth protected the flanks of Lee's infantry in the Bristoe Campaign and fought in the so-called Buckland Races in October. It clashed with Meade's troops again in the Mine Run Campaign at the end of November, before going into winter quarters. It did not see action again until fifty-three of its soldiers helped turn back the Kilpatrick-Dahlgren Raid on Richmond, February 29–March 2, 1864. About that time, Roberts received promotion to major, with rank to date from February 18.

Roberts's next major action came in opposition to General Ulysses S. Grant's Overland Campaign (May–June 1864). As the newly appointed general in chief of the U.S. Army, Grant had taken overall command of the Army of the Potomac, retaining Meade in tactical command. Grant's objectives were to attack Lee's army with unceasing pressure and force it back toward Richmond and ultimate surrender. The Federals sustained large casualties at the Battles of the Wilderness (May 5–6), Spotsylvania Court House (May 7–19), and Cold Harbor (June 1–3). Grant's campaign, however, eventually forced the Army of Northern Virginia into entrenchments at Petersburg.

During the campaign, the Nineteenth reported the enemy's movements and protected the infantry's flanks. At the fighting at Yellow Tavern on May 11, the regiment was not engaged on the field but skirmished with the rear guard of General Philip H. Sheridan, whose cavalry was attempting to raid Richmond. Although the Confederate cavalry thwarted Sheridan's raid, Stuart received a mortal wound in the struggle. Roberts himself suffered a slight head wound at Haw's Shop on June 3. He was admitted to a hospital in Richmond but returned to duty within a few days. On August 19, Roberts was promoted to colonel and given command of the Nineteenth North Carolina.

He led the regiment into battle at Reams's Station on August 25, when he dismounted his troops and successfully attacked a Union position. The regiment also participated in the famed Hampton's Beefsteak Raid of September 11–16, in which the Confederate cavalry secured a large herd of cattle for the starving soldiers of the Army of Northern Virginia. Roberts's continued leadership of his troops in the Richmond and Petersburg area led to his promotion to brigadier general and command of a brigade in William H.F. Lee's division on February 23, 1865. At age twenty-three, he became the youngest general commissioned in the Confederate army. Tradition reports that Robert E. Lee gave him his own gauntlets to commemorate his promotion and courage.

The last major combat for Roberts came at the Battle of Five Forks (April 1), in which the Federals achieved a victory and turned Lee's right flank. That Union success allowed Grant's men to break through the Confederates' defenses and force them to evacuate their trenches at Petersburg. Roberts's seriously depleted brigade then accompanied the Army of Northern Virginia's retreat westward. Roberts, whose brigade at the time included only five officers and eighty-five men, was present when Lee finally surrendered to Grant at Appomattox Court House on April 9.

Following the surrender and his parole, Roberts returned to Gates County and took up farming. He served as a delegate from Gates County in the state Constitutional Conventions of 1868 and 1875 and then in the state legislature. He was elected state auditor in 1880 and was reelected four years later, but he declined to run for another term in 1888. President Grover Cleveland then appointed him consul to Victoria, British Columbia, and he held that position for several years before returning to Gates County and farming. Following a fall at home, he died in a Norfolk hospital on March 27, 1910, and was buried at the Old City Cemetery in Gatesville. Shortly after the war, he had married Eliza Roberts (of no kinship). They had two children, but both died in childhood.

Alfred Moore Scales

1827–1892
Brigadier General

Alfred Moore Scales was born in Reidsville, Rockingham County, North Carolina, on November 26, 1827. He attended the Caldwell Institute in Greensboro and in 1845 entered the University of North Carolina at Chapel Hill, where he studied law but did not graduate. He read law with Judge William H. Battle and was admitted to the bar in 1852, the same year that he became solicitor for Rockingham County. He served in the state legislature for two terms and then in the U.S. House of Representatives, 1857–59.

Shortly before North Carolina's secession from the Union on May 20, 1861, he joined the Thirteenth Regiment North Carolina Troops (originally formed as the Third Regiment North Carolina Volunteers) as a private in Company H and was immediately elected captain. The regiment soon went into camp at Suffolk, Virginia. In October, Scales received promotion to colonel and command of the Thirteenth Regiment. The previous commander, William Dorsey Pender, had been transferred. Scales became ill soon afterward and remained in his quarters for part of the winter.

He recovered in time to lead his regiment in the Peninsula Campaign (March–July 1862), in which the Confederate army, originally led by General Joseph E. Johnston, opposed the Army of the Potomac, commanded by General George B. McClellan. The Federals had landed on the coast of Virginia and began an advance along the peninsula between the York and James Rivers toward the Confederate capital at Richmond. Scales and his troops saw action as Johnston's force retreated up the peninsula.

At the Battle of Seven Pines on May 31, Johnston was wounded and succeeded by General Robert E. Lee, who reorganized the Confederates defending Richmond into the Army of Northern Virginia and launched a series of attacks known as the Seven Days Battles (June 25–July 1) to drive McClellan's army from eastern Virginia. The Confederate assaults resulted in the Army of the Potomac's withdrawing to a heavily fortified position at Malvern Hill. On July 1, Lee ordered an all-out attack on that Union position. It proved costly in the large number of casualties among his soldiers and failed to dislodge the defenders. Nevertheless, McClellan ordered an evacuation from the peninsula.

Following the Battle of Malvern Hill, Scales collapsed from exhaustion and went on convalescent leave. He returned to duty in mid-November, in time to lead his troops at the Battle of Fredericksburg on December 13. In that battle, the Army of the Potomac, then commanded by General Ambrose E. Burnside, attempted a poorly conceived attack on the Confederates' formidable defenses on Marye's Heights. The result was tremendous casualties for the Federals. After its victory, the Army of Northern Virginia went into winter quarters but was soon on the march again.

At the Battle of Chancellorsville (May 1–3, 1863), it dealt another defeat to the Army of the Potomac, then led by General Joseph Hooker. On the last day, Scales received a bullet wound in the thigh but remained in the field until he had to retire because of a loss of blood. Two of his men carried him to the rear on a stretcher. Chancellorsville was probably Lee's greatest victory, although he lost his valuable subordinate General Thomas J. (Stonewall) Jackson, who was mortally wounded accidentally by North Carolina troops. Scales recuperated at home for some weeks and received promotion to brigadier general on June 13. His new brigade included the Thirteenth, Sixteenth, Twenty-second, Thirty-fourth, and Thirty-eighth Regiments North Carolina Troops. It was part of General Pender's division in General A.P. Hill's corps.

In late June, Lee's army began an invasion of Pennsylvania. That initiative would end in disaster for it at the Battle of Gettysburg (July 1–3), when the Army of the Potomac, then commanded by General George G. Meade, inflicted heavy losses and turned back the ill-conceived and ill-fated charge by Lee's troops against Cemetery Ridge on the last day. On July 1, the first day, Scales's brigade went into action at Seminary Ridge and was "all but wrecked in the fighting." Scales later described that combat:

> *We pressed on until coming up with the line in our front....I received orders to halt, and wait for this line to advance. This they soon did, and pressed forward quick time....I again ordered an advance, and, after marching one-fourth of a mile or more, again came upon the front line, halted and lying down. The officers on this part of the line informed me that they were without ammunition, and would not advance farther. I immediately ordered my brigade to advance. We passed over them, up the ascent, crossed the ridge, and commenced the descent just opposite the theological seminary. Here the brigade encountered a most terrific fire of grape and shell on our flank, and grape and musketry in our front. Every discharge made sad havoc in our line, but still we pressed on at a double-quick until we reached the bottom....Here I received a painful wound from a piece of shell, and was disabled. Our line had been broken up, and now only a squad here and there marked the place where regiments had rested.*

As the Confederates retreated, the wounded Scales rode in an ambulance with Pender, who soon died of his wound. Scales, however, recovered at Winchester, Virginia, and returned to his brigade to fight in Lee's opposition to General Ulysses S. Grant's Overland Campaign (May–June 1864). Grant had recently been appointed general in chief of the U.S. Army. He took personal charge of the Army of the Potomac, with Meade in tactical command. His objectives were to apply constant pressure on the Army of Northern Virginia, force it back toward Richmond, and effect its eventual surrender. The Union troops sustained heavy casualties at the Battles of the Wilderness (May 5–6), Spotsylvania Court House (May 7–19), and Cold Harbor (June 1–3), but they ultimately forced Lee's army into trenches around Petersburg. At the Wilderness on May 6, Scales's brigade broke and fell back in disorder. On May 12, at the famed Mule Shoe at Spotsylvania, the brigade performed well in a successful Confederate counterattack, and it helped hold the line at Cold Harbor.

The brigade left its trenches at Petersburg to take part in a successful attack on a Federal position at Reams's Station on August 25. As Grant continued to extend his siege lines in an effort to flank Lee's defenses, Scales's troops participated in a number of small actions around Petersburg. On April 1, 1865, the Federals finally broke Lee's line, and the Army of Northern Virginia abandoned its entrenchments and retreated westward. At that time, Scales was at home on convalescent leave. He was therefore not present at Appomattox Court House when Lee surrendered to Grant on April 9.

After the war, Scales moved to Greensboro and resumed the practice of law. A Democrat who had been an elector for John C. Breckinridge in the presidential election of 1860, he served in the state legislature during Presidential Reconstruction and then in the U.S. Congress from 1875 to 1884. In Washington, he chaired the Committee on Indian Affairs and investigated fraud in the Indian Bureau. He then answered the Democratic Party's call to stand for election as North Carolina governor, and he served in that office from 1885 to 1889. Afterward, he returned to Greensboro and became president of the Piedmont Bank. He continued to endure bad health, and visits to northern medical specialists did not improve his condition. He died in Greensboro on February 9, 1892, and was buried at Green Hill Cemetery.

Scales married twice. Before the war, he married Margaret Smith of Louisiana, but she refused to move to North Carolina, and the state legislature granted him a divorce. In 1862, he married Katherine Henderson of North Carolina. They had no children but adopted a niece.

Thomas Fentress Toon

1840–1902
Brigadier General (Temporary)

Thomas Fentress Toon was born in Columbus County, North Carolina, on June 10, 1840. He attended local schools and then Wake Forest College. On the day that the Tar Heel State seceded from the Union, May 20, 1861, he volunteered for Confederate service as a private. When the Twentieth Regiment North Carolina Troops (originally designated the Tenth Regiment North Carolina Volunteers) was organized on June 18 at Fort Johnston near Smithville (present-day Southport) in Brunswick County, he was elected first lieutenant of Company K. He became captain about a month later.

The infantry regiment remained in the lower Cape Fear region of North Carolina until June 14, 1862, when it transferred to Richmond, Virginia, to join the brigade of General Samuel Garland, in the division of General D.H. Hill. Colonel Alfred Iverson Jr. commanded the regiment.

The Twentieth North Carolina soon went into action during the Seven Days Battles (June 25–July 1), when General Robert E. Lee commanded his newly formed Army of Northern Virginia in a counterattack against the U.S. Army of the Potomac, led by General George B. McClellan. The Federals had landed on the coast of Virginia and were advancing toward the Confederate capital at Richmond along the peninsula between the York and James Rivers. At the Battle of Gaines Mill on June 27, the Twentieth Regiment assaulted a Union artillery position near a swamp in the vicinity of Cold Harbor. As the attack began, wrote historian Douglas Southall Freeman, "the Carolinians were in full cry; a little longer and they were upon the guns. The instant Hill saw his men struggling with the Federal artillerists, he unloosed every regiment on the southern edge of the swamp....Soon the Federals were wavering, were breaking." The Tar Heels did not hold the captured guns. But Hill—not known for giving praise—remarked that "no doubt a greater loss was saved to the Division in its advance by this gallant attack." Toon himself was wounded at Gaines Mill but soon returned to duty.

Iverson was more seriously wounded, however, and Lieutenant Colonel Franklin J. Faison took temporary command of the regiment. At the Battle of Malvern Hill on July 1, the Twentieth advanced on the heavily fortified Federal defenses but was forced to halt, take cover, and then retreat. Although Lee's Seven Days Campaign resulted in the withdrawal of McClellan's army from the peninsula, casualties were high. At the Battles of Gaines Mill and Malvern Hill, the regiment lost 93 men killed, 281 wounded, and 6 missing.

During the Second Battle of Manassas (or Bull Run) on August 29–30, in which Lee's main force defeated the U.S. Army of Virginia, led by General John Pope, the Twentieth North Carolina remained in the area around Richmond. Then Garland's brigade, including Toon's regiment, became heavily engaged at South Mountain on September 14 with an element of McClellan's army. Garland was mortally wounded in the fighting, and Colonel Duncan McRae of the Fifth North Carolina State Troops temporarily took over the brigade.

Under the new brigade commander, the Twentieth Regiment—then commanded by Iverson, who had recovered from his wound—fought in the bloody Battle of Sharpsburg (or Antietam), Maryland, on September 17. Halted by McClellan's army at Sharpsburg, Lee's troops retreated into Virginia. On November 1, Iverson received promotion to brigadier general and command of Garland's old brigade, replacing McRae, who had resigned from the army.

At the Battle of Fredericksburg in December, the Army of Northern Virginia devastated the Union ranks during an ill-conceived charge on the strong Confederate defenses on Marye's Heights by the Army of the Potomac, then led by General Ambrose E. Burnside. Toon's regiment saw little action, however, although it endured heavy artillery fire. On February 26, 1863, Toon was promoted to colonel and placed in command of the Twentieth North Carolina.

He led the regiment in the Battle of Chancellorsville (May 1–4), where Lee's troops inflicted another crushing defeat on the Army of the Potomac, then commanded by General Joseph Hooker. The Twentieth North Carolina had fifteen killed, sixty-seven wounded, and eighteen missing in the fighting. Early on the morning of May 3, Toon received a wound, and by ten o'clock, he had suffered two more, which made it necessary for him to leave the battlefield and temporarily give up command.

But he was back at the head of his soldiers in time for the Army of Northern Virginia's invasion of Pennsylvania in late June. At that point, his regiment and Iverson's brigade were in the division of General Robert E. Rodes, who had taken over from Hill, and in the corps of General Richard S. Ewell, who had replaced General Thomas J. (Stonewall) Jackson, killed at Chancellorsville. At the ensuing Battle of Gettysburg (July 1–3), the Army of the Potomac, then led by General George G. Meade, inflicted a major defeat on Lee's army. Toon and his troops were heavily involved in the combat and fought in rearguard actions as the Confederates retreated across the Potomac River. In the Gettysburg operations, the regiment lost twenty-nine men killed and ninety-three wounded. Because of his failed performance in the battle, Iverson was transferred, and General Robert Daniel Johnston took over command of the brigade. Toon's Twentieth Regiment took part in a number of movements and skirmishes in Virginia before becoming engaged in the Mine Run Campaign in late November and early December. It then went into winter quarters.

Toon's next major action came in the Overland Campaign (May–June 1864) of General Ulysses S. Grant, who had recently become general in chief of the U.S. Army. Grant personally led the Army of the Potomac, with Meade in tactical command, in a relentless attempt to drive the Army of Northern Virginia back toward Richmond and secure its eventual surrender. The Federals sustained high casualties at the Battles of the Wilderness (May 5–6), Spotsylvania Court House (May 7–19), and Cold Harbor (June 1–3), but they finally forced Lee's army into trenches at Petersburg. As the campaign unfolded, Johnston's brigade was transferred from the division of General Rodes to the division of General John Brown Gordon. Before the war ended, the brigade, including Toon's regiment, would come under the divisional command of several other generals, including Jubal A. Early, Stephen Dodson Ramseur, and John Pegram.

Toon and his troops fought at the Wilderness and Spotsylvania. A bullet wounded him in the leg at Spotsylvania on May 12, but he remained absent from duty for only a few days. Johnston was wounded in the head the same day and then hospitalized at Charlotte, North Carolina. On May 31, Toon received temporary promotion to brigadier general and command of the brigade, which he led at Cold Harbor.

Johnston returned to command the brigade, and Toon returned to the Twentieth Regiment and fought in Lee's Second Corps, then led by Early, in the Shenandoah Valley Campaign (August 7, 1864–March 2, 1865). In that campaign, Early won a number of victories and even threatened the U.S. capital at Washington before he was ultimately defeated by General Philip H. Sheridan and the U.S. Army of the Shenandoah.

As the result of either his wounds or illness, Toon was in the general hospital at Richmond from December 9 to 28, 1864. He then returned to duty with his troops in the entrenchments around Petersburg, As he stood on the breastworks at Hare's Hill to rally his men on March 25, he was seriously wounded. He was convalescing at a home in Petersburg when Lee finally surrendered to Grant at Appomattox Court House on April 9.

After the war, Toon returned to Columbus County, where he engaged in teaching and farming and also worked for the Atlantic Coast Line Railroad. He served as mayor of Fair Bluff and county school examiner. He was a member of the state House of Representatives in 1881–82 and the state Senate in 1883–84. He moved to nearby Robeson County in 1891 and taught at Robeson Institute. In 1900, he was elected North Carolina's superintendent of public instruction and moved to Raleigh. Along with Governor Charles Brantley Aycock and prominent educator and college president Charles Duncan McIver, he labored to improve literacy in the state. Toon contracted pneumonia in November 1901 and remained seriously ill for some time. He had shown a slight improvement when he died of heart failure at home in February 1902. He was buried at Oakwood Cemetery in Raleigh.

In 1866, Toon had married Carrie E. Smith of Fair Bluff, and they had two sons and three daughters. Following her death, he married Rebecca Cobb Ward in 1891.

Robert Brank Vance

1828–1899
Brigadier General

R obert Brank Vance was born at Reems
Creek, near Asheville in Buncombe
County, on April 24, 1828. His brother,
Zebulon Baird Vance, two years younger,
became North Carolina's governor during
the Civil War. Robert Vance received a
limited formal education at home and in
local schools. As a young man, he served as
clerk of the Buncombe County Court. He
gave up that office to become a merchant in
Asheville in 1858.

With the outbreak of the Civil War and
North Carolina's secession and alliance with
the Confederacy, Vance received an appointment as colonel of the Twenty-
ninth Regiment North Carolina Troops, which formed in Buncombe
County in September 1861. The regiment traveled to Raleigh in early
November and acquired arms, equipment, and uniforms. It left the state
capital on November 25 for detached service in east Tennessee. Five days
later, it arrived at Haynesville Depot, near Jonesboro, on the East Tennessee
Railroad and set about its mission of operating against a pro-Union faction
and establishing Confederate authority in the area.

In February 1862, the regiment reported to the garrison commanded by
Colonel James E. Rains at Cumberland Gap, where it helped turn back a Federal

attack led by General George W. Morgan. When General Carter L. Stevenson took command of the Confederate detachments at Cumberland Gap, Vance's regiment was assigned to his brigade, which repelled another Union assault on April 29. Morgan's men then flanked the Confederates, however, and forced them to abandon their position and fall back to Bean's Station.

By that time, the Confederate forces in east Tennessee had come under the overall command of General Edmund Kirby Smith. In the reorganization, Stevenson became commander of a division, and Rains took over his old brigade. Vance's Twenty-ninth remained under their command. In August 1862, Kirby Smith moved his troops to cooperate with the army of General Braxton Bragg in an attack on the Federals holding Cumberland Gap, who were part of the army of General Don Carlos Buell. During that operation, the Twenty-ninth North Carolina skirmished with the enemy at Tazewell and then was detached from the main Confederate body and deployed at nearby Baptist Gap.

Unable to capture Cumberland Gap, Kirby Smith moved nine thousand of his men northward on August 24 to support Bragg's invasion of Kentucky. Stevenson's division, including the Twenty-ninth, remained behind in Tennessee. On August 30, Kirby Smith's force drove off green Union troops at Richmond, Kentucky, and then marched into Lexington. That resulted in the Federals' evacuation of Cumberland Gap, which was then occupied by Stevenson's division, including Vance's regiment.

Buell's subsequent defeat of Bragg at the Battle of Perryville in October forced the Confederates to retreat into Tennessee. There, Vance and his regiment were deployed at various locations before moving to Murfreesboro on December 10. Earlier that month, Kirby Smith had been reassigned, and Rains's brigade, including the Twenty-ninth North Carolina, was transferred to the division of General John P. McCowan, in the corps of General William J. Hardee, in Bragg's newly formed Army of Tennessee.

At the Battle of Murfreesboro (or Stone's River) on December 31– January 2, the Army of the Cumberland, led by General William Rosecrans, defeated Bragg's army, which retreated to Shelbyville and then Chattanooga. In the fighting, the Twenty-ninth had about sixty men killed and wounded. Rains was killed on December 31, and Vance temporarily commanded the brigade, receiving praise for his performance.

Vance soon fell victim to typhoid fever. During his illness, he was promoted to brigadier general to rank from March 4, 1863. Upon his recovery, he took command of a separate military district in western North Carolina created by the Confederate War Department. His mission was to repulse Federal raids into western North Carolina and to assist the main

Confederate force in Tennessee with raids of his own. Vance's command, never large, included several companies of Cherokee Indians in the regiment (sometimes called a legion) of Colonel William Holland Thomas.

In January 1864, General James Longstreet ordered Vance to push across the Great Smoky Mountains and aid the Confederate effort in Tennessee. As he crossed into Tennessee, Vance divided his expedition into two parts. He sent Thomas's troops and 350 men under Colonel James L. Henry toward Gatlinburg. He himself, with two hundred men, advanced toward Sevierville. En route on January 13, he and his soldiers captured a Union supply train. On the way back into western North Carolina with the supplies, he stopped at Cosby Creek, expecting to be reinforced there by Henry and Thomas. Vance did not post pickets, and he and fifty of his soldiers were easily captured by the Fifteenth Pennsylvania Cavalry, commanded by Colonel William Palmer. A soldier in the Fifteenth Pennsylvania described the incident: "With a yell as the mountains have never heard before or since," he recalled, "our command fell upon the Confederates in the center, forcing them up and down the stream in direst confusion, with little or no resistance."

U.S. authorities imprisoned Vance first at Nashville, Tennessee, and then Louisville, Kentucky. He was later moved to Fort Chase, Ohio, and finally to Fort Delaware. His brother, Governor Zebulon B. Vance, blamed his capture on Henry and Thomas and attempted, unsuccessfully, to have them court-martialed. In large part because of his own earlier kind treatment of a Union prisoner, General Vance was treated well while imprisoned. His captors allowed him to purchase and distribute clothing for other Confederate prisoners of war. On March 14, 1865, he received parole and permission to return to North Carolina, with the stipulation that he never rejoin the fighting.

With his U.S. citizenship restored after the war, Vance was elected to Congress in 1872 and served six terms. As a member of a number of committees, he obtained federal appropriations for his mountain district, including funds for daily mail delivery and the dredging of the French Broad River. In 1884, President Grover Cleveland appointed him assistant commissioner of patents, a position he held through the president's first term. Vance was active in a number of fraternal organizations and the Methodist Episcopal Church. He also wrote poetry and served in the state legislature from 1893 to 1896. He died at his farm near Asheville on November 28, 1899, and was buried at Riverside Cemetery in the city.

In 1851, Vance had married Harriet V. McElroy, daughter of Home Guard general John W. McElroy, and they had six children, four of whom survived to adulthood. She died in 1885, and he married Lizzie R. Cook seven years later.

William Henry Chase Whiting

1824–1865
Major General

W illiam Henry Chase Whiting was born on
March 22, 1824, at Biloxi, Mississippi.
His father, Levi, was an officer in the U.S. Army
and a native of Massachusetts. The younger
Whiting was exceptionally intelligent. He was
educated in Boston and at Georgetown College
in Washington, D.C., where he completed the
four-year course in two years. He then graduated
first in his class from the U.S. Military Academy
at West Point in 1845, with the highest scholastic
record ever achieved up to that time.

As it did with all its best academy graduates,
the U.S. Army assigned the newly commissioned
Lieutenant Whiting to the engineers, and he oversaw work on harbors and
fortifications in California and along the Gulf and south Atlantic coasts. He
also acted as lighthouse engineer for North and South Carolina, improved
the passage from Albemarle Sound to the Atlantic Ocean, and served for
two years on the lower Cape Fear River. He received a promotion to captain
in 1858 and was on duty at Savannah, Georgia, when that state, as it seceded
and joined the Confederacy, seized the U.S. military posts in the port city in
January 1861.

Despite his Northern background and family ties, Whiting embraced
secession and the Southern cause. He resigned his U.S. commission

in February 1861 and soon joined the staff of General Pierre G.T. Beauregard as engineer at Charleston, South Carolina, with the rank of major. He then functioned briefly as inspector general for North Carolina before being appointed chief of staff to General Joseph E. Johnston, commanding Confederate forces in Virginia. He played a significant role in the seizure of arms and equipment from the Federal arsenal at Harpers Ferry and in transferring Johnston's troops from the Shenandoah Valley to the First Battle of Manassas (or Bull Run) on July 21, 1861. At that battle, the Confederate forces of Beauregard, reinforced by Johnston's units coming from the west, defeated the U.S. army led by General Irvin McDowell in the first large engagement of the war. Because of his performance as Johnston's chief engineer at Manassas, Whiting was promoted to brigadier general. Johnston reported that he "was invaluable to me for his signal ability in his profession and for his indefatigable activity before and in the battle."

As Confederate commander in Virginia, Johnston led his divisions in the first battles of the Peninsula Campaign (March–July 1862). His mission was to oppose the Army of the Potomac, commanded by General George B. McClellan, which had landed on the coast of Virginia and was advancing toward the Confederate capital at Richmond by way of the peninsula between the York and James Rivers. Although a brigadier general, Whiting commanded a division during that campaign. He fought at the Battle of Seven Pines (May 31–June 1), where Johnston was wounded. General Robert E. Lee took over his command, reorganizing it into the Army of Northern Virginia.

Under Lee's leadership, Whiting led his division in the Seven Days Battles (June 25–July 1), in which Lee counterattacked McClellan with the objective of driving him away from Richmond and off the peninsula. The Confederates' persistent assaults ultimately forced the Army of the Potomac to a heavily fortified position on Malvern Hill. On July 1, Lee ordered a full attack on the position. That ill-conceived assault produced heavy Confederate casualties and failed to dislodge the Federals. In Whiting's division during the Seven Days Campaign, General John B. Hood's brigade sustained the most losses, with 623 men killed, wounded, or missing. Nevertheless, McClellan called off his offensive and evacuated his army from eastern Virginia.

Following Malvern Hill, Whiting sent some letters of complaint to Lee. It is not certain what his complaints were, but possibly they were associated with his not being promoted to major general and given permanent division command. Lee responded soothingly by telling him to "forget them, General; do not let us recollect unpleasant things; life is very short. We have so much to do. We can do so much good, too, if we are not turned aside. Everything will come right in the end."

Whiting had already shown his temperamental and argumentative nature in an earlier quarrel with the War Department when it attempted to assign him troops from Mississippi. In September 1861, President Jefferson Davis had instructed Johnston to brigade soldiers from the same state together. Being from Mississippi himself, he wanted the men from that state assigned to the brigades of Whiting and General Richard Griffith, both natives of Mississippi. An angry Whiting refused to comply with what he considered a bad idea. He wrote to the War Department that the president's plan was "a policy as suicidal as foolish...inconceivable folly...solely for the advancement of log-rolling, humbugging politicians. I will not do it." An incensed president ordered the War Department to give Whiting a "stern rebuke." Only support by Johnston saved him from a worse outcome. But a mutual dislike between Davis—never one to accept criticism from anybody—and Whiting never healed. The president denied a request for his promotion to major general in May 1862.

After the Seven Days Battles, Whiting did not continue to campaign with the Army of Northern Virginia. He went on sick leave, and when he returned to duty in October, Lee had decided to give his former division command to Hood. According to historian Douglas Southall Freeman, Lee "knew better than did most officers the deep pessimism of Whiting's nature, but he also knew that Whiting had exceptional ability as an engineer." Lee therefore urged the War Department to send him to "some other post where engineering skill was needed." Whiting received orders to report to the secretary of war in Richmond and in November was transferred to North Carolina to command the District of the Cape Fear, with headquarters at Wilmington. He finally was appointed major general on April 22, 1863.

But Whiting's critical, outspoken personality continued to keep him in constant controversy. He quarreled with local officials at Wilmington and with other army and naval commanders on the coast. He and Governor Zebulon B. Vance developed a long-running enmity when he tried to shut down the state's saltworks on the lower Cape Fear. Rumors began to circulate that Whiting was sometimes intoxicated on duty, and he accused Vance of spreading such stories. The governor denied the charge, and the relationship between the two temperamental men continued to worsen. Whiting petitioned for transfer back to the Virginia front.

In May 1864, his requests were fulfilled when Beauregard asked for him to be attached to his command. At that time, General Ulysses S. Grant, newly appointed general in chief of the U.S. Army, had launched his Overland Campaign (May–June). He took personal command of the Army of the Potomac, with its former leader, General George G. Meade, as a subordinate and began a relentless series of attacks to force the Army of Northern Virginia back toward Richmond and effect its eventual surrender. The Federals sustained heavy casualties at the Battles of the Wilderness, Spotsylvania Court House, and Cold Harbor but ultimately forced Lee's army into trenches at Petersburg.

During the campaign, Beauregard, in command at Petersburg, attacked the army of General Benjamin F. Butler and managed to pin it up at Bermuda Hundred, a large neck of land between the James and Appomattox Rivers south of Richmond. At the Second Battle of Drewry's Bluff, where Beauregard attacked Butler on May 16, Whiting, leading a small division, failed to get his force into battle on time at Port Walthall Junction. That led to rumors that he had been drunk again. Although they were probably unfounded, Beauregard did upbraid him for his failure. Whiting then returned to Wilmington.

In September 1864, an exasperated Governor Vance ask Lee to transfer Whiting from North Carolina. Lee sympathized with Vance and admitted that Whiting's irascibility made him difficult to work with, but he expressed confidence in the general's engineering skill.

Still seething from Whiting's insults, however, President Davis did not regard him so kindly and placed his friend General Braxton Bragg in charge at Wilmington. Bragg dismissed Whiting's worries about the number of troops available to defend Fort Fisher against a Federal attack. A joint army-navy assault, commanded by General Butler and Admiral David D. Porter, came on December 24, and it failed. But a renewed attack, with army operations then led by General Alfred H. Terry, succeeded in capturing the fort on January 15, 1865. During the battle, Bragg remained in Wilmington and refused to release from the town the 6,500 troops led by General Robert F. Hoke, who had been sent to help defend the fort. Whiting, however, rushed to the fort, where he fought bravely as a volunteer. As he led a countercharge, he was wounded twice in the right leg. One bullet passed through his hip, causing a severe injury. With the fall of Fort Fisher, the Federals occupied Wilmington, the last blockade-running port of the Confederacy, as the war was coming to an end.

William Henry Chase Whiting

Whiting was taken prisoner and sent to Fort Columbus on Governors Island in New York Harbor. There he wrote a report stating that Fort Fisher could have been held if Bragg had committed Hoke's troops from Wilmington. Whiting's wounds did not prove fatal, but he suffered from depression and severe diarrhea and died on March 10, 1865, only weeks before the war ended. He was buried first at Greenwood Cemetery in Brooklyn but was reinterred at Wilmington's Oakdale Cemetery in 1900. In 1857, he had married Katherine Davis Walker of Wilmington. They had no children.

Cadmus Marcellus Wilcox

1824–1890
Major General

Cadmus Marcellus Wilcox was born on May 29, 1824, in Wayne County, North Carolina. While still a child, he moved with his parents to Tipton County, Tennessee. He attended the University of Nashville before entering the U.S. Military Academy at West Point. He graduated from the academy in 1846, near the bottom of his class. During the Mexican-American War (1846–48), he won distinction for leading a charge at Chapultepec. For his bravery, he received a brevet to first lieutenant and an assignment as aide to General John A. Quitman.

Wilcox served next in Florida and then as assistant instructor of infantry tactics at West Point from 1852 to 1857. He subsequently traveled for a year in Europe in an attempt to improve his poor health. In 1859, he published a training manual titled *Rifles and Rifle Practice*, and a year later, he translated *Austrian Infantry Evolution of the Line*. Having been promoted to captain in late December 1860, he was on duty in New Mexico when the Civil War began. He resigned his U.S. commission on June 8, 1861, and accepted an appointment as colonel of the Ninth Alabama Infantry. He led the regiment at the First Battle of Manassas (or Bull Run) in Virginia on July 31. In that first major action of the war, Confederate troops under General Pierre G.T. Beauregard defeated the Union army commanded by General Irvin McDowell.

On October 21, 1861, Wilcox received promotion to brigadier general, with command of a brigade in the expanded division of General James Longstreet, under the overall Confederate commander in Virginia, General Joseph E. Johnston. His next combat came during the Peninsula Campaign (March–July 1862), in which Johnston attempted to halt the advance of the Army of the Potomac, led by General George B. McClellan, toward Richmond. The Federals had landed on the coast of Virginia and were moving on the Confederate capital along the peninsula between the York and James Rivers. Wilcox and his brigade saw action at Williamsburg, where his performance validated his promotion to brigadier, as Johnston withdrew his forces toward Richmond. While the campaign continued, Wilcox's brigade fought at the Battle of Seven Pines (May 31–June 1), where Johnston was wounded and General Robert E. Lee took charge of his command. Lee reorganized the Confederates into the Army of Northern Virginia and launched the Seven Days Battles (June 25–July 1) in a counterattack to drive the Army of the Potomac from the peninsula. Lee's persistent attacks ultimately drove the Federals to a strongly fortified position on Malvern Hill. On July 1, an ill-conceived assault brought heavy Confederate casualties and failed to dislodge the Union troops. Nevertheless, McClellan terminated his campaign and soon removed his army from Virginia. In the Seven Days Battles, Wilcox's brigade sustained the highest casualties of any brigade in Longstreet's command.

The next major combat for Wilcox and his brigade was at the Second Battle of Manassas (or Bull Run) on August 29–30. It resulted in another victory for the Army of Northern Virginia, this time over the U.S. Army of Virginia, under the leadership of General John Pope. Lee followed his success at Manassas with an invasion of Maryland. At the ensuing Battle of Sharpsburg (or Antietam) on September 17, McClellan's Army of the Potomac halted the Confederates' advance and forced their retreat across the Potomac River. Wilcox, though, was absent during the Maryland operation, and Colonel Alfred Cumming temporarily commanded his brigade.

He was back at the head of his troops in time for the Battle of Fredericksburg in December. A month earlier, Lee had organized his army into corps, and Longstreet acquired the First Corps. Wilcox had hoped for a promotion to major general and command of a division in the new corps. But Longstreet, whom Wilcox strongly disliked, passed him over, leaving him leading a brigade in the division of General Richard H. Anderson. At Fredericksburg, the Army of Northern Virginia scored a one-sided victory over the Army of the Potomac, this time led by General Ambrose E. Burnside. With little chance of success, the Federals charged strong Confederate defenses at Marye's Heights and suffered a huge number of casualties. Wilcox's brigade served on the left of Anderson's line but did not play a large role in the fighting.

Wilcox's greatest achievement in the war came during the Chancellorsville Campaign (April–May 1863). As Lee moved a large portion of his army from Fredericksburg to confront the Army of the Potomac, then led by General Joseph Hooker, Wilcox aggressively closed a Federal penetration of the Confederates' rear guard at Salem Church. That effort helped to ensure victory for the Army of Northern Virginia at the Battle of Chancellorsville on May 1–4. Wilcox managed to carry it off even though he suffered from dysentery at the time. But despite the skill and success of his maneuver, he was once again passed over for promotion to major general and division command.

Following his win at Chancellorsville, Lee decided to invade Pennsylvania. That decision led to the Battle of Gettysburg (July 1–3) and a major defeat for the Army of Northern Virginia by the Army of the Potomac, then led by General George G. Meade. On the second day of the battle, Anderson's division independently assaulted the left center of a Union line that had formed in a peach orchard. The attack accomplished little and was very costly for the Confederates. Of the 4,100 soldiers in Anderson's three brigades engaged in the action, 1,561 were killed, wounded, and missing. For some years afterward, Wilcox expressed his resentment and anger at Anderson, whom he blamed for the loss of 577 soldiers in his brigade. "I am quite certain," he declared after the war, "that Gen'l A never saw a foot of ground on which his three brigades fought on the 2nd of July. I may be wrong [about] Gen'l A, but I always believed that he was too indifferent to his duties at Gettysburg." Wilcox's remaining troops participated in the infantry's famed and disastrous charge on the Federal position on Cemetery Ridge on July 3. In the attack, his men marched behind the advancing right column led by General George Pickett, but they never reinforced Pickett's division, which was virtually annihilated.

On the day after its catastrophe at Gettysburg, Lee's army began retreating into Virginia. On July 18, General William Dorsey Pender, who commanded a division in the corps of General A.P. Hill, died of a wound received at Gettysburg. Wilcox was then transferred to command Pender's division, and he received official promotion to major general on August 3, 1863. He was down ill for a time the following winter.

Wilcox and his new division were engaged on a significant scale in the Overland Campaign (May–June 1864) of General Ulysses S. Grant, who had recently become general in chief of the U.S. Army. Placing himself in overall command of the Army of the Potomac, with Meade as a subordinate, Grant launched a persistent campaign to drive the Army of Northern Virginia back toward Richmond and effect its surrender. His troops suffered large casualties at the Battles of the Wilderness (May 5–6), Spotsylvania Court House (May 7–19), and Cold Harbor (June 1–3), but they eventually drove Lee's army into entrenchments at Petersburg. At the Wilderness, Wilcox's division fought stubbornly along the Orange Plank Road, where it constituted half of the Confederate strength. At Spotsylvania, it protected the right of the Confederate line near the important crossroads. At Cold Harbor, it was also stationed on the right of the line.

Wilcox's division then went into the Petersburg trenches, along with the rest of Lee's army, where the general was again ill in March 1865. On April 1, the Federals broke through Lee's line, and the Army of Northern Virginia abandoned its trenches and fled westward. Wilcox's division effectively protected the army's rear as it withdrew. Its flight ended on April 9 when Lee surrendered to Grant at Appomattox Court House, where Wilcox was present. Following the formal signing of the surrender, Wilcox—who had been a groomsman at Grant's wedding before the war—visited briefly with the Union general, along with a number of other Confederate officers.

After the war, Wilcox, who never married, moved to Washington, D.C., where he lived with his older brother's widow and two children. The brother, a former Texas congressman, had died in the last months of the war, and Wilcox had taken over the care of his family. Wilcox turned down commissions in the Egyptian and Korean armies. President Grover Cleveland appointed him chief of the Railroad Division of the General Land Office in 1886, and he held that office until his death on December 2, 1890. The pallbearers at his funeral included both Union and Confederate generals. Wilcox was buried at Oak Hill Cemetery in Washington. He had written a massive (711-page) history of the Mexican-American War, which his niece published posthumously in 1892.

Wilcox proved himself an able, if not brilliant, general who, according to historian James I. Robertson Jr., was "a tough fighter who, once a military objective had been fixed, drove toward that point unswervingly." He was well liked by his soldiers and fellow Confederate officers. Wilcox also had a number of prewar friends among U.S. officers, and his West Point classmates included Hill, McClellan, and Pickett. At six feet tall, he probably cut an odd image in battle, wearing a short, rounded jacket and straw hat and sitting astride a white pony. His men sometimes referred to him as "Old Bill Fixing" because of his nervous, fussy nature.

Bibliography

Allardice, Bruce S. *More Generals in Gray*. Baton Rouge: Louisiana State University Press, 1995.

Anderson, Jean Bradley. *The Kirklands of Ayr Mount*. Chapel Hill: University of North Carolina Press, 1991.

Ashe, Samuel A., Stephen B. Weeks, and Charles L. Van Noppen, eds. *Biographical History of North Carolina*. 8 vols. Greensboro, NC: Charles L. Van Noppen, 1905–7.

Barefoot, Daniel W. *General Robert F. Hoke: Lee's Modest Warrior*. Winston-Salem, NC: John F. Blair, 1996.

Barrett, John G. *The Civil War in North Carolina*. Chapel Hill: University of North Carolina Press, 1963.

Boatner, Mark M., III. *The Civil War Dictionary*. New York: David McKay, 1959.

Buell, Thomas B. *The Warrior Generals: Combat Leadership in the Civil War*. New York: Three Rivers Press, 1997.

Casstevens, Frances H. *The 28th North Carolina Infantry: A Civil War History and Roster*. Jefferson, NC: McFarland Publishers, 2008.

Clark, Walter, ed. *Histories of the Several Regiments and Battalions from North Carolina in the Great War, 1861–'65*. 5 vols. Raleigh: State of North Carolina, 1901.

Cole, J. Timothy, and Bradley R. Foley. *Collett Leventhorpe, the English Confederate: The Life of a Civil War General, 1815–1889*. Jefferson, NC: McFarland Publishers, 2007.

Current, Richard M., et al., eds. *Encyclopedia of the Confederacy*. 4 vols. New York: Simon and Schuster, 1993.

Evans, Clement A., ed. *Confederate Military History: A Library of Confederate States History in Twelve Volumes, Written by Distinguished Men of the South*. 12 vols. Atlanta, GA: Confederate Publishing Company, 1899.

Faust, Patricia L., et al., eds. *Historical Times Illustrated Encyclopedia of the Civil War*. New York: Harper and Row, 1986.

Freeman, Douglas Southall. *Lee's Lieutenants: A Study in Command*. 3 vols. New York: Charles Scribner's Sons, 1942–44.

Gallagher, Gary W. *Stephen Dodson Ramseur: Lee's Gallant General*. Chapel Hill: University of North Carolina Press, 1985.

Gragg, Rod. *Confederate Goliath: The Battle of Fort Fisher*. New York: HarperCollins, 1991.

Harrell, Roger H. *The 2nd North Carolina Cavalry*. Jefferson, NC: McFarland Publishers, 2004.

Hess, Earl J. *Lee's Tar Heels: The Pettigrew-Kirkland-MacRae Brigade*. Chapel Hill: University of North Carolina Press, 2002.

Hill, Michael, ed. *The Governors of North Carolina*. Raleigh: North Carolina Office of Archives and History, 2007.

Inscoe, John C., and Gordon B. McKinney. *The Heart of Confederate Appalachia: Western North Carolina in the Civil War*. Chapel Hill: University of North Carolina Press, 2000.

Johnson, Robert Underwood, and Clarence Clough Buel, eds. *Battles and Leaders of the Civil War*. 4 vols. New York: Century, 1887–88.

Johnston, Frontis W., and Joe A. Mobley, eds. *The Papers of Zebulon Baird Vance*. 2 vols. to date. Raleigh: North Carolina Office of Archives and History, 1963–.

Jones, Carroll C. *The 25ᵗʰ North Carolina Troops in the Civil War: History and Roster of a Mountain-Bred Regiment*. Jefferson, NC: McFarland Publishers, 2009.

Jordan, Weymouth T., Jr., and Gerald W. Thomas. "Massacre at Plymouth: April 20, 1864." *North Carolina Historical Review* 72 (April 1995): 125–93.

Manarin, Louis H., comp. *A Guide to Military Organizations and Installations, North Carolina, 1861–1865*. Raleigh: North Carolina Confederate Centennial Commission, 1961.

Manarin, Louis H., Weymouth T. Jordan Jr., and Matthew Brown, comps. *North Carolina Troops, 1861–1865: A Roster*. 17 vols. to date. Raleigh: North Carolina Office of Archives and History, 1966–.

Parks, Joseph H. *General Leonidas Polk, C.S.A.: The Fighting Bishop*. Baton Rouge: Louisiana State University Press, 1962.

Poteat, R. Matthew. *Henry Toole Clark: Civil War Governor of North Carolina*. Jefferson, NC: McFarland Publishers, 2009.

Powell, William S., ed. *Dictionary of North Carolina Biography*. 6 vols. Chapel Hill: University of North Carolina Press, 1979–96.

Robertson, James I., Jr. *General A.P. Hill: The Story of a Confederate Warrior*. New York: Random House, 1987.

Samito, Christian G. "'Patriot by Nature, Christian by Faith': Major General William Dorsey Pender, C.S.A." *North Carolina Historical Review* 76 (April 1999): 163–201.

Trotter, William R. *Bushwhackers: The Civil War in North Carolina, the Mountains*. Winston-Salem, NC: John F. Blair, 1988.

———. *Ironclads and Columbiads: The Civil War in North Carolina, the Coast*. Winston-Salem, NC: John F. Blair, 1989.

Warner, Ezra J. *Generals in Gray: Lives of the Confederate Commanders.* Baton Rouge: Louisiana State University Press, 1959.

The War of the Rebellion: A Compilation of the Official Records of the Union and Confederate Armies. 128 vols. Washington, D.C.: Government Printing Office, 1880–91.

Waters, W. Davis. "'Deception Is the Art of War': Gabriel J. Rains, Torpedo Specialist of the Confederacy." *North Carolina Historical Review* 66 (January 1989): 29–60.

Welsh, Jack D. *Medical Histories of Confederate Generals.* Kent, OH: Kent State University Press, 1995.

Wilson, Clyde N. *Carolina Cavalier: The Life and Mind of James Johnston Pettigrew.* Athens: University of Georgia Press, 1990.

Woodworth, Steven E. *Jefferson Davis and His Generals: The Failure of Confederate Command in the West.* Lawrence: University of Kansas Press, 1990.

About the Author

J oe A. Mobley teaches in the Department of History at North Carolina State University in Raleigh. This is his fifth book related to the American Civil War.

Visit us at
www.historypress.net